Make, Sew and Mend

Traditional Techniques to Sustainably Maintain and Refashion Your Clothes

Bernadette Banner

PAGE STREET
PUBLISHING CO.

PAGE STREET
PUBLISHING CO.

First published in 2022 by
Page Street Publishing Co.
27 Congress Street, Suite 1511
Salem, MA 01970
www.pagestreetpublishing.com

Distributed by Macmillan, sales in Canada by The Canadian Manda Group.

26   25   24   23   22   3   4   5

ISBN-13: 978-1-64567-486-3
ISBN-10: 1-64567-486-X

Library of Congress Control Number: 2021939500

Cover and book design by Rosie Stewart for Page Street Publishing Co.
Photography by Bernadette Banner
Additional design elements from Shutterstock and Creative Market

Printed and bound in the United States

Dedication

For Bertha Banner (no relation)

Contents

Introduction

The realization has occurred to me that, for all the sewing projects I have documented online, rarely do I take a moment to stop and explain the basics: how to start and end the thread, why I've cut pattern pieces in certain directions and what is meant by such words as *bias* and *fell*. So, while it has become fairly clear over the years that the online videos are meant primarily as mainstream entertainment and something nice to look at, if you actually want to know the gritty details, you will probably require something a bit more practical. And so, here we are. It's weird seeing you here in this strange new format, but we're going to have a good time.

This whole online hand sewing business began as a personal endeavor to learn more about the history of humans through an attempt to reconstruct the clothes that they wore. But very quickly I began to understand that, despite the technological advancements that now make certain aspects of modern society easier and more efficient, sometimes that efficiency develops to a fault: Modern manufacturing favors speed over craft, quantity over quality. Just because we do things faster or cheaper or with fancy machines nowadays doesn't necessarily mean that we do things better—and indeed, the definition of the word *better*, in this case, is neither an objective one, nor does it qualify a singular goal. Certainly our capability for mass production today is better, but speed often results in a sacrifice of quality; cheapness, a sacrifice of fair worker compensation and quality of material; overproduction, a sacrifice

of mindful consumption. In our efforts to progress into "better," the 21st century has seen the explosive rise of a trillion-dollar fashion industry responsible for more greenhouse gas production than all the shipping and aviation industries combined.[1]

None of this is to say that the textile industries in the centuries before our present one were perfect—the issue of underpaid garment workers is certainly nothing new to modern fast fashion. The discrepancy between the labor involved in the production of good-quality clothing and the price many people are able to pay, coupled with the stigma in recent centuries that sewing is "women's work" and thus of lesser value, has never been a problem fully resolved. But here lies the advantage of the present: We have the ability to pick out from the past all the things that did work, whilst examining those that didn't, and adjust our solutions accordingly. This has since become a habit of mine, when in need of a solution to a problem: to look back at the long list of solutions to similar problems that history has already laid out for us. What similar struggles did our ancestors face, and what solutions were devised? What can we learn from the methods, trials, experiments, mistakes and successes of the past, so as to solve our own problems more thoroughly and efficiently? The quantity of data we have for forming new solutions is greater now than it has ever been.

In the days before mass manufacture, clothing tended to be obtained in one of three ways— either it was self-made, was made for the

wearer by another person (whether family or on commission from a dressmaker or tailor) or obtained secondhand, be that through purchasing, trading or handing down amongst family members. It wasn't until the Industrial Revolution in the mid-19th century that western Europe and North America began seeing the normalization of clothing produced in standard sizing on a mass-manufacture scale, made by workers trained in small portions of the manufacturing process and who would never come into contact with the wearer. Even so, the scale of mass manufacture tended to be of a regional or national capacity rather than the global levels of distribution that mass-manufactured products experience today. Conscious attitudes toward the purchasing of new clothing, even in the form of ready-to-wear, carried through into the 20th century. One 1916 home manual instructs its readers that "Each garment in one's wardrobe, or the materials for its construction, should be selected with the following consideration:

1. The need for its purchase;

2. The use to which it must be put;

3. Its durability;

4. Its suitability to the wearer;

5. Its cost in relation to the allowance."[2]

This advice on purchasing clothing responsibly is provided alongside practical sewing, mending, patterning and maintenance advice, implying that the consumer of ready-to-wear garments was still expected to have an understanding of how clothing was mended and made.

Apart from the very upper classes, who could afford to wear a gown only once or twice, there was no expectation that new clothing had to be bought by the season or that outfits couldn't be repeated multiple days in the week. This was, granted, slightly obligatory due to the amount of labor required of hand weaving and hand making clothes, particularly in the preindustrial eras, so each garment was inherently more costly. Most people knew how to sew, or knew someone who knew how to sew. Clothing wasn't made by invisible hands in faraway lands as is much of our clothing in Western society today, meaning that, historically, the labor required in garment production was inescapable in the mind of the wearer. This absence of societal expectations and pressures toward consumption, particularly of fashion and textiles, laid the groundwork for a lifestyle operating on slow rather than fast fashion.

If we are seeking to avoid buying into the system of mass manufacture and opt instead for the practice of slow fashion, we can assess our options similarly to how our ancestors might have done: We can thrift our clothes, buying secondhand from vintage or thrift shops, or swap with family or friends. We can make clothes ourselves or alter garments that already exist. The time involved in this endeavor, as well as the personal expenditure on materials, tend to incline us toward a more careful use of materials as well as a slower rate of acquisition; and a thorough understanding of the garment allows us to mend, alter or refashion it with greater confidence in the future. Finally, we can have clothing made for us via the business of custom tailoring. While this latter option is an excellent way to obtain well-crafted and unique garments, it is not the most widely financially accessible and, for the purposes of this text, we will be focusing on the previous options that allow you to put these sewing techniques into practice for yourself.

Through my efforts to explore original-practice garment construction for my own research, I have learned that, though these methods are now much forgotten, they still produce strong, durable, long-lasting and beautifully crafted items. As history so kindly teaches us, you don't need to have any fancy machinery to be able to take your wardrobe, quite literally, into your own hands. Hand sewing gives us the ability to produce just as strong and durable work as machines can, as proven during the centuries preceding the increased adoption of the sewing machine in the 1860s. Hand-sewn clothing was lived in, worked in, mended, refashioned and could last the wearer for decades. Hand sewing is, inevitably, quite a bit slower than machine sewing, so do feel free to supplement these techniques with modern conveniences if you wish. It is my goal with this text to offer a starting point should you wish to take control of the clothes you wear—to make them more uniquely you through the upcycling, alteration, mending, refashioning or construction of full garments that have value to you; to give you the ability to make do and mend so that your clothes last you as long as possible.

Bernadette Banner

Feature: Dandy Wellington

One of the scariest things a person can do is embrace and embody their own personal style. It's terrifying to present yourself to the world so uncompromisingly "you." In an effort to waylay the matter, most will say: "I don't really have a style" or "I just want to be comfortable," but simply put, style is personal. It is a window to how you see the world and how you'd exist in it. For these reasons, personal style is so important and powerful. It's an affirmation of your true inspiration, what brings you joy and who you really are. Here's how I found my personal style:

I was born to a life overflowing with books, art, cinema and song in a former speakeasy in Harlem, New York City. Though I could not have known it at the time, that setting's historic significance was distinct and would affect me fully. For within those walls and without, my mother made it her business to immerse me in facts of my ancestors' struggles and the fruits of their resilience. In the fact that the cause and effect of history is inextricably linked to our culture; and that culture is connected to our style. Endless love, music and the lessons history has to offer are the lens through which I see the world, and for me, there was no better backdrop than Harlem.

Harlem is a powerful place in which to grow up. A neighborhood of awe-inspiring history that has played host to some of the most influential figures and crucial characters in Black culture. From Louis Armstrong to Langston Hughes to Jacob Lawrence to Zora Neale Hurston, the list goes on; and with Harlem as my playpen, my childhood was imbued with the rich cultural history it has to offer. Even now, in my everyday life I see the influences of having grown up listening to the great performances of Nat King Cole, Marian Anderson, Duke Ellington and others. Their talent, their work ethic and the joy they brought to the world in the face of seemingly insurmountable obstacles and equally effortless style was revolutionary. How could I not want to emulate Ellington in his silk, plush top hat and tail or white double-breasted dinner jacket? When listening to the heavenly horn of Louis Armstrong, I found myself, not just tapping my toes but searching for a pair of plus fours just so I could be like my hero. Their talent helped inspire me to be a performer. Their presence inspired me to embrace my true personal style.

The key to personal style is inspiration. Not from a passing fad or the look for the week but deep, robust, sapid inspiration. The kind of inspiration that creeps into your dream and brings you such joy in the night that you wake searching for a pen to write it all down. Inspiration can serve as an entry point to the most elegant of rabbit holes. The more time you spend with it, the more specific and nuanced it will become. My inspiration connects to my roots and is a North Star to my true self. It's a product of a childhood full of the art and culture that brought me joy. For joy is the goal. What inspires you?

—Dandy Wellington (he/him)

Preparing
Materials

Choosing Materials

Perhaps the biggest factor in the outcome of a garment is determined at stage one: Regardless of sewing skill, the success or failure of a project begins, primarily, with the choice of cloth. This doesn't need to be the most expensive or luxurious fabric option—it just needs to be the most appropriate one for the unique requirements of the garment.

Every fabric behaves differently, depending on the structure, weight and fiber content of the cloth; this includes how it drapes, how it appears, whether it has moisture-wicking or temperature-controlling properties or whether it has textures that can be soft or abrasive. Certain fabrics are ideal for tailored garments, whereas others are better for flowing silhouettes. There is no such thing as a "good" or a "bad" fabric objectively, simply the more—or less—suitable fabrics for a particular job.

Thus the first step in making a garment is to determine what you wish to make, and for what purpose it is to be worn. An undergarment? An outer garment? Something to be worn around the house, making comfort a top priority? Will this garment need to withstand heat, moisture or frequent washing? Will it need to be seen up close? Does it need to stand out at a distance? Will it need to stretch or be alterable, or will it need to be structured, to build out or reshape the natural figure?

Let's start with the fiber content, as this will play a substantial role in determining the qualities of the finished garment: whether it will be easy to wash, will be comfortable in the heat or will keep you warm in winter.

Linen: Made from flax fibers, linen is washable and durable to hard wear. Per the nature of plant fibers, linen absorbs moisture, so it will keep the skin clean and dry, and is the best fiber choice for hot weather. For this reason, linen was used for centuries as the undermost layer worn next to the skin; its absorbability protected the outer, less washable layers of clothing from coming into contact with oils on the body. Linen is a naturally antibacterial fiber, meaning that it does not provide a suitable environment in which bacteria can easily grow, so it helps inhibit body odor and keeps the skin cleaner for longer periods of time. Undyed, linen garments could most easily withstand the rigors of regular washing, and as linen softens with regular washing, the garments become wonderfully comfortable over time.

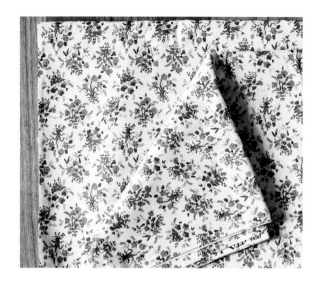

Cotton: Likewise a plant fiber, cotton is also a breathable and absorbent material that performs well in hot weather. It is hard wearing and can be machine-washed and dried, making for a very durable and practical material. Cotton is often the least expensive natural fiber material to buy, so it is an excellent choice for those wishing to work with natural materials on a budget; cotton muslin, the unbleached, untreated form of cotton cloth, is so cheap as to be the material of choice for mockups, or prototype versions of a garment. Cotton ranges dramatically in weight and thus can serve a range of purposes: drill, duck or canvas, for example, are heavy, hard-wearing cloths that will be durable enough for rucksacks and workwear; cotton voile or lawn, on the other hand, are diaphanous and delicate enough for a cool summer frock.

Wool: Wool has been a staple in textile production for thousands of years; many breeds of domestic sheep today require annual shearing so as not to become unhealthily overgrown, making wool a highly symbiotic and sustainable fiber choice especially when sourced from small-scale manufacturers. A single fleece contains various qualities of fiber, with those closer to the body of the sheep being softer (and often more costly) than the rougher fibers on the outside, so wool isn't only the heavy, scratchy cloth we often think it is. Worsted wool cloth is made from long wool fibers that have been combed both to remove the short fibers and to align them so that they run parallel to one another. This produces a much lighter, finer, softer cloth than wools made from woolen yarns, which produce heavier, thicker cloths. Summer-weight wools are woven loosely to produce an airy, breathable fabric, and contrary to popular belief, these will keep you much cooler in the hot weather than silk or synthetic fibers will.

 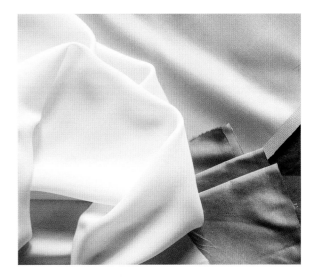

Wool can be a costly fabric in general, so it is often blended with synthetic fibers to reduce yardage cost while still maintaining the natural insulating properties of wool. Washing wool is generally not advised, as it's prone to shrinkage and felting if agitated or heated too much, so it's best to gently hand wash or dry clean. Certain tightly woven worsted wools can withstand machine washing, although a test swatch of this should be run through the wash before it's made up into a garment that will need to be washed. When washing wool, be sure to submerge the material entirely rather than allowing water to run over it, as this can cause uneven shrinkage.

Silk: Silk is a protein fiber made primarily from the larvae cocoon of the *Bombyx mori*, commonly known as a silkworm. The fiber has a natural sheen to it, although silk textiles vary in luster depending on the weave and treatment of the fabric. Silk was historically—and often still is—costly, so modern silks are often supplemented with synthetic fibers to reduce cost. Natural silk is extremely heat-retentive, so is not a good choice for high-temperature wear. It may be dry-cleaned but should not be washed with water, as water can alter the sheen and crispness of the silk fibers and cause staining if dried unevenly. If the fabric must be wet, ensure that the entire yardage is evenly and entirely soaked, then dried evenly and thoroughly so as not to result in water spots.

Artificial silks, such as rayon and viscose, are also made from cellulose fibers and thus are naturally more breathable than polyester (petroleum-based) silks while also generally looking more like natural silk; these are often significantly cheaper than natural silks, so are an excellent alternative for the discerning seamster on a budget.

Polyester: Synthetic materials, such as polyester, spandex, acrylic and nylon, are petroleum-based fibers; as this means that they're effectively plastic, these have very low breathability and should be avoided for use in hot-weather garments. Synthetic fibers are very easy to produce and thus can be very inexpensive to buy, and are often blended with natural fibers to reduce the cost of more expensive silks or wools, or to add stretch to fabrics. These materials tend not to crease as easily as natural linen or cotton fabrics, so are preferred by those who wish for machine-washable garments with reduced ironing time.

Identifying Fiber Content

If you are unsure of the fiber content of a particular fabric in your possession, burn and bleach tests can help determine or estimate the fiber content of your material. This is especially important if you plan to dye your fabric, as natural fiber materials will take most dyes easily, while synthetic materials will resist most dyes; you'll need to obtain specialty poly-dyes when working with synthetics. Do keep in mind that some materials are sized during manufacturing, meaning that the yarn or the fabric itself has had a sizing treatment applied to strengthen the finished cloth. This process may affect the test results.

Please note: These tests require the use of open flame and chemical bleach. Exercise caution, operate in a fireproof environment and employ fire and chemical safety measures.

Be aware that oil-based materials such as polyester and acrylic can flare up very quickly when exposed to flame. Minors should not attempt these tests without the supervision of an adult.

Preparation: Cut a small sample of the fabric to be tested, no more than 2 inches (5 cm) square.

Wool sample

You will need: A fireproof surface, such as a pan or metal sink; a match, candle or lighter; a small, bleach-safe dish; chlorine bleach; and gloves or tweezers for handling bleached materials. Do also be sure to have some water nearby when using an open flame.

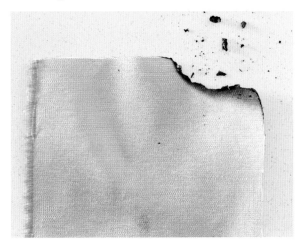

Silk sample

Cotton sample

Linen sample

Wool sample 10 seconds submerged

Synthetic sample

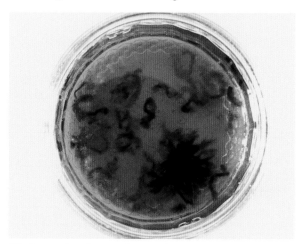

Wool sample 1 hour submerged, partially disintegrated

Rayon sample

The burn test: Over a fireproof surface, hold one end of your test swatch with tweezers. Light one edge of the material with a match, lighter or candle. Observe the flame, rate of burn, smoke, odor and ash or residue.

The bleach test: Using a bowl or shallow dish, submerge your test swatch in bleach. Let stand for a minimum of one hour. Observe any disintegration of the material. This is a good test to perform if you know the natural protein fiber of a material but wish to test whether it has been blended with synthetics, as protein fibers will disintegrate when treated with bleach, whereas synthetic and cellulose fibers will not.

Examples

Burn test: Ignites and burns quickly, may flare, produces a gray smoke and continues to glow after extinguishing; smells of burning paper and crumbles into fine gray ash unless fabric has been treated, in which case the ash may be black.

Bleach test: Will not disintegrate.

Result: Cotton (cellulose fiber)

Burn test: Ignites and burns slightly slower than cotton but still burns quickly; smells of burning paper and produces a fine, gray ash.

Bleach test: Will not disintegrate.

Result: Linen (cellulose fiber)

Burn test: Ignites slowly, smolders, then self-extinguishes when the flame is removed; produces dark smoke and extinguishes on its own. Smells strongly of burnt hair and produces a soft char that crushes into dark, gritty ash.

Bleach test: Will disintegrate.

Result: Wool (protein fiber)

Burn test: Difficult to burn, smolders, curls away from the flame; produces little to no smoke and self-extinguishes. Smells of burnt hair and produces a bead that is easy to crush into a gritty ash.

Bleach test: Will disintegrate.

Result: Silk (protein fiber)

Burn test: Ignites and burns very quickly; does not continue to glow after extinguishing. Smells of burning paper and produces a feathery, gray ash.

Bleach test: Will not disintegrate.

Result: Rayon (manufactured cellulose fiber)

Burn test: Ignites easily but burns briefly. Shrinks from flame and melts; produces a slightly sweet chemical odor and melts into a plastic bead that cannot be easily crushed.

Bleach test: Will not disintegrate.

Result: Polyester (petroleum-based synthetic fiber)

Burn test: Ignites easily but burns briefly. Shrinks from flame and drips as it melts, self-extinguishing. Smells vaguely of celery and produces no ash but a hard, gray bead that cannot be easily crushed. *Fumes are hazardous.*

Bleach test: Will not disintegrate.

Result: Nylon (petroleum-based synthetic fiber)

Burn test: Ignites easily but burns briefly. Shrinks from flame and melts; can drip while burning. Smells of vinegar, leaves no ash and produces hard, black beads that cannot be easily crushed. *Fumes are hazardous.*

Bleach test: Will not disintegrate.

Result: Acetate (manufactured protein fiber)

Burn test: Flares and burns quickly; shrinks from flame and drips as it melts; self-extinguishes; smells chemical, vaguely fishy and does not produce ash but a hard, irregular bead that is difficult to crush. *Fumes are hazardous.*

Bleach test: Will not disintegrate.

Result: Acrylic (petroleum-based synthetic fiber)

If your fabric is a blend of fibers, your results may involve several of the qualities described here; for example, a cotton-polyester blend will give off an odor of burning paper and may produce some ash, but will also harden into a plastic bead when cooled.

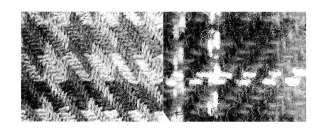

Anatomy of the Cloth

It is important first to understand the basic structure of the cloth so that we can better understand how the fabric will behave in various uses, although the intricacies of weaving are so vast and complex as to require an entire text of their own. I will leave the technical details and the infinite varieties of weave structure to the more comprehensive sources[3] while providing here an introductory anatomy of fabric through which we can begin to predict how the cloth will behave when we go to sew it.

Textiles are made—if they aren't already workable in their natural forms, such as with leathers, furs and PVCs ("pleathers")—through a variety of methods: weaving, knitting and felting.

Weaving is the most common form of textile production, whereby yarns spun from various fibers are intersected to form a length of cloth. This is commonly achieved on a loom: The vertical yarns (the warp) creating the framework through which the horizontal yarns (the weft) are to pass through. These warp yarns are the

stronger, since it is the weft that must pass over and under the warp yarns. A selvedge is produced along the length of the warp as the weft yarns pass back and forth, and this is how you'll be able to tell each grain apart: The yarns parallel to the selvedge will be your straight of grain, or your warp grain; the edge that has been cut from the bolt of the fabric will be your cross grain, or the weft.

This leaves the third direction, the bias, which is the diagonal angle between the straight and cross grains. The true bias lies at exactly the 45-degree angle between the warp and weft, and the fabric will stretch slightly when pulled in this direction. (In Britain and some parts of Europe, the bias is known as *the cross*, a term that is worth keeping in mind when reading British English texts, such as Janet Arnold's *Patterns of Fashion* series, but which I will be avoiding use of here so as not to confuse it with the cross grain.)

Silk duchess satin

A basic 1:1 weave fabric, with one weft yarn passing over one warp yarn and then under the next

A twill weave, in which a weft yarn passes over one warp yarn and then under two warp yarns, with this pattern slightly offset from row to row, to produce the diagonally ribbed texture

A satin, with weft yarns passing over four or more warp yarns at a time to expose the glossy shine of the fibers (in this case silk, although satins can be woven from any fiber)

A brocaded fabric with additional yarns woven in to create a figured pattern in the cloth

A velvet fabric with warp yarns cut to form the standing pile; i.e., what makes velvet fluffy

Weave patterns can vary greatly and do not always stick to a 1:1, over-one-under-one configuration; sometimes a weft yarn may pass over two or three warp yarns at a time, producing a twill weave that appears as a series of diagonal ridges; sometimes a silky weft floats over four or more warp yarns to produce the shimmery surface of a satin weave. Sometimes many additional yarns can be incorporated, woven on complex jacquard looms to produce elaborately figured jacquards and brocaded fabrics. Warp or weft yarns can be looped or doubled and then cut to form the soft pile that defines velvet (warp cut pile) or velveteen (weft cut pile); the textile possibilities are numerous and endless. Regardless of which fabric you have chosen to work with, if it is a woven fabric, it is always essential to pay attention to the three grain directions before cutting out.

Grain is one of the most important factors to pay attention to when working with fabric, as a fabric will behave differently based on how it's cut—and an unintentional misuse of grain can be of great disadvantage. For example, accidentally cutting a structured skirt on a slight bias will cause it to droop or stretch in a manner that you might not have intended.

As a general rule (and I say "general" as rules are made to be consciously broken on occasion), the straight of grain should run vertically on the body in traditional dressmaking and tailoring.

This is because our clothing tends to need to hang straight, and the vertical inclination of the straight grain complements the vertical influence of gravity. It should be noted that this gravitational pull likewise affects the bias grain, so that bias-cut areas of a garment set vertically will be inclined to stretch over time. When working with vertical bias seams, such as cutting a skirt or long dress on the bias, the panels should be hung for a few days to allow this bias to stretch naturally. The excess length can then be cut off to achieve a level hem.

Strategic use of the bias can also be a great advantage, as historical makers were well aware in the days before spandex and elastic: Socks, hose, sleeves and certain bodice panels were sometimes cut on the bias to allow for a bit of natural stretch in close-fitting garments. This, incidentally, is why we have diagonally oriented argyle socks—before knitting, these would have been ordinary non-stretch tartan cloth cut on the bias.

Knit fabrics, such as jersey, feature natural stretch due to the interlocking loop nature of the individual yarns. Knitting is an alternate method of fabric production to weaving, and can be achieved with any fiber type. Felting, on the other hand, is yet another method of making cloth, and is achieved by interlocking the scaly protein fibers (such as those from sheep or alpaca) with heavy agitation to form a solid thickness of matted material. Both knitted and felted materials are less prone to fraying (although knits will unravel), and, in the case of felted materials, do not have grain lines by which a fabric will behave differently from one direction to the next.

The center back seam of this skirt has been cut on the bias without sufficient pre-hanging time, so has stretched to form an uneven hemline.

A knit fabric: A single yarn looped together to form a textile

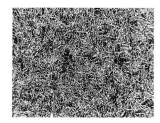

A felted fabric: Not made from spun yarns woven together, but instead from individual, interlocking, short-staple fibers

Preparing the Fabric

As a general rule, fabric should be washed according to the manner in which it will be treated as a complete garment before the making process begins. This not only removes any manufacturing treatments that the fabrics may have been subjected to, but it also gives the fabric a chance to shrink *before* you make it into a garment that is supposed to fit you. (Yes, this exposes the nefarious doings of some clothing manufacturers who decline to prewash material before production because it makes their jobs easier, leaving you to deal with the consequences.) As a general rule, garments made from washable materials that you plan to clean regularly will need to have their fabric prewashed before you can begin cutting out.

How to Prewash

Linen: Machine wash, line dry. Tumble dryers can break down the flax fibers more quickly.

Cotton: Machine wash and tumble dry.

Wool: May be hand washed gently, but do not agitate or machine wash as it may begin to felt. The safest method to pretreat wool is to roll it up in a damp sheet, leave overnight to soak, then steam dry with a hot iron. This will wash and preshrink it without felting it.

Silk: It is best not to wash silk. If necessary, it may be dry-cleaned, but theoretically your final silk garment will not be washed and so prewashing won't be strictly necessary. If silk must be wet, be sure to wet the entire length of fabric (or the entire garment) and line dry evenly to avoid water staining.

Synthetics: Machine wash; tumble dry and iron on low settings to avoid melting. Always test heat on a swatch before applying to the real fabric or garment.

Before throwing your fabric in the wash, be sure that any raw edges are roughly finished off or you may lose a few inches to unraveling. This can be done by quickly running it through an overlocker (serger) or double folding and basting with very long running stitches just to hold the ends temporarily. (See pages 55 and 56 if you need detailed instruction on running stitches and basting.)

After washing, the yardage should be pressed to smooth out any wrinkles and to straighten the grain, which may have warped during washing. While pressing, the iron should be moved either in straight vertical or horizontal motions, along the straight or cross grain of the material, but not diagonally as these movements may cause the fabric to stretch and shift off grain.

Should any parts of the yardage require straightening, simply give it a couple of hard tugs along the bias to shift it back into place.

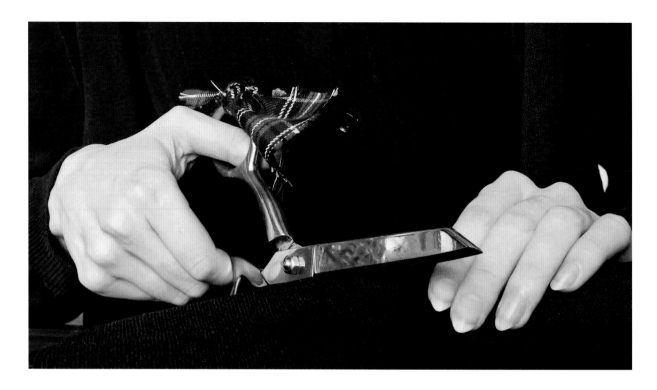

Cutting Out

Before cutting out your pattern pieces, it is first important to be aware of your seam allowance situation, particularly if the pattern you're using is not one you've drafted yourself. Patterns are drafted either *net*, meaning that the pattern shape is the distilled shape of the garment piece itself *without seam allowance included*; or the pattern shape may be drafted with the seam allowance incorporated into the shape itself. Most commercial patterns are drafted with seam allowance, whereas most historical patterns (e.g., those from primary sources, in drafting manuals, theatrical costume patterns or such texts as Janet Arnold's *Patterns of Fashion* series) are drafted net.

Commercial pattern instructions specifying the ⅝-inch (1.5-cm) seam allowance included in the pattern shapes

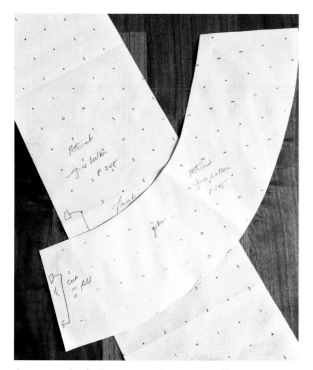

A pattern drafted net, or without seam allowance included

Sewing with an antique machine, which does not have seam allowance gauging next to the foot. Seam allowance wider than the width of the foot itself will need to be marked.

Each system has benefits and drawbacks depending on your intended method of sewing, whether that will be by hand or by machine. For example, patterns incorporating seam allowance make the cutting-out process much quicker, but only if you will be using a modern sewing machine with seam allowance gauging at the foot, which will allow you to measure in the appropriate seam allowance from the edge of the fabric. If you plan to sew by hand or with an antique sewing machine, however, you will need to take a ruler and manually measure in the seam allowance to mark the net-pattern line, as you will need to have a line to stitch along so as to get the correct garment size.

A pre-marked seam line to guide a row of hand stitches

The benefit of using net patterns—and the reason these were commonly used historically and are still used today by theatrical costume and bespoke garment makers—is you get to decide how much seam allowance you wish to add. Sometimes you may want a narrow seam allowance to make a narrow felled finish, or sometimes you may want lots of extra seam allowance if your fabric is prone to fraying or if you want to allow for some fitting room in tricky places, such as armscyes (where a sleeve joins the garment). Having lots of extra seam allowance can also be useful if you're prone to size fluctuation, so your garment can easily be let out and taken in as necessary. A pattern without seam allowance included will also save you the time of measuring in the actual seam lines if you plan to sew by hand or with an antique machine.

Single or Double?

It is common practice to fold the width of the material when cutting two pieces of a symmetrical garment so that both pieces may be cut at once. This is reasonable for stable fabrics, such as sturdy cottons or wools, but fabrics that have a tendency to move about—such as loose silks or linens—will need to have each piece cut individually. This way, you can ensure that your grain lines are straight, as these are not easy to verify on the underside piece of double-folded yardage. Grain lines are *very* important to the behavior of your final garment, so a bit of time and attention spent here will do you great service in the long run.

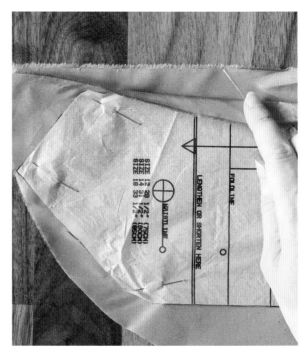

Fabric cut double, two layers at once

Fabric cut single, only one layer at a time

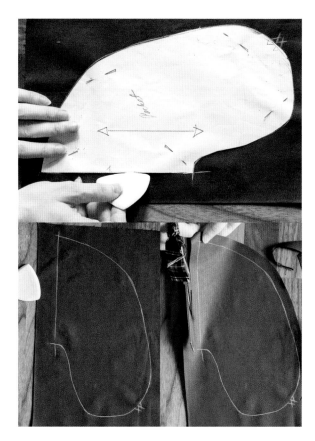

For cutting out patterns with seam allowance:
Simply lay the pattern piece onto the fabric along the appropriate grain line and weight or pin it into place. Cut directly along the edge of the pattern paper.

If hand stitching a seam allowance pattern:
Once the shape is cut, you will need to go through and measure the seam allowance width from the edge of the panel in, marking a stitching line either with pencil or with chalk. This step is not necessary for machine sewing if your machine has a seam allowance gauge on the foot.

For cutting out net patterns: Lay the pattern piece onto the fabric according to the appropriate grain line and weight or pin it into place. Mark with pencil or chalk directly around the edge of the pattern paper. You can then either measure out your desired seam allowance width around the pattern shape, or just estimate this by eye when cutting; precise seam allowance measurements are not strictly necessary since you'll be following the marked stitching line rather than using the edge of the material as a gauge for the stitching line. Cut out the pattern shape, either along your marked seam allowance line (*not* the stitching line), or simply cut a small distance away from your stitching line, estimating your seam allowance by eye.

Thread Marking

Sometimes a simple marked line isn't sufficient for a particular job and it'll be well worth making the additional effort to trace over these lines with long basting stitches. The first instance in which thread marking may be preferred is when working with disappearing pens or powdered marking substances such as chalk or charcoal on certain materials; wools and felts especially will shed the dust quickly, erasing your important stitching lines. Although this is great for producing final garments free of marking lines, sometimes a piece will need to be handled frequently—or may sit in the UFO (unfinished object) pile for some time before you get around to stitching it—giving the markings enough time to lose their visibility.

Some finer fabrics, such as silk taffetas, do not have this problem and will retain chalk markings more permanently, so do a test on your fabric to see whether any additional marking will need to be done.

The other instance in which thread marking can be useful is if you'll need to be able to see your stitching line on both sides of the fabric: for example, if you're going to be stitching multiple layers of material together, or if you plan to French seam your garment. In this instance, a thread-marked stitching line will show through on both sides of the material, giving you ample reference as you work.

Thread marking along the stitching line. It is best to do this just at the edge or 1 mm away from your actual marked line so that the thread doesn't get caught in your final seam and will be easier to remove.

A thread marked pocket shape

Thread marking is done by running a very long basting stitch approximately 1 mm parallel to your marked stitching line. The goal is speed here, not strength, as these will be removed later, so longer stitches are preferred—and the threads are not anchored at the starting or finishing points. The thread markings are worked not on top of the actual stitching line, as this will then get stitched into your actual seam and make the basting threads difficult to remove later, but ever so slightly onto the seam allowance so as not to catch in your stitching needle. Do be sure also to mark any balance marks, darts or tucks, and to extend all marking lines about an inch (2.5 cm) past the line so that your corners and intersections are very clear.

Remember: When laying your patterns and cutting, *always pay attention to your grain lines!* Commercial patterns will provide lines and arrows telling you in which direction to cut your pieces: Grain lines on patterns should be aligned to the straight grain, or along the selvedge. Always measure from the selvedge to the grain line and make sure that this measurement is exactly the same on both ends of the grain line to be sure that your pattern piece is lying perfectly on-grain. If you're working with a self-drafted pattern or a historical pattern in which you are responsible for determining the grain line yourself, you can use your newfound knowledge of grain behavior (see page 21) to decide which will be the best grain for cutting. The straight grain will be the strongest and the cleanest when hanging, so is best used vertically on the body; the bias will provide stretch, which can be used to ease areas, such as tight sleeves or tight-fitting legwear, or to wrap smoothly and snugly around the body, such as in some corset panels or the fronts of 18th-century bodices. Do always ensure that straight grain instructions are always followed when specified, as even slight deviations onto the bias can cause your garment to hang in unintended ways.

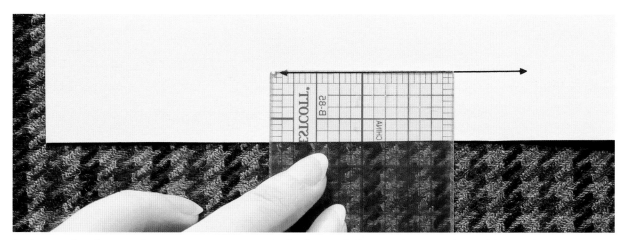

Make sure that the grain lines on your pattern perfectly align with the straight grain of your fabric, either by measuring to the selvedge or to a straight line in the weave of the material.

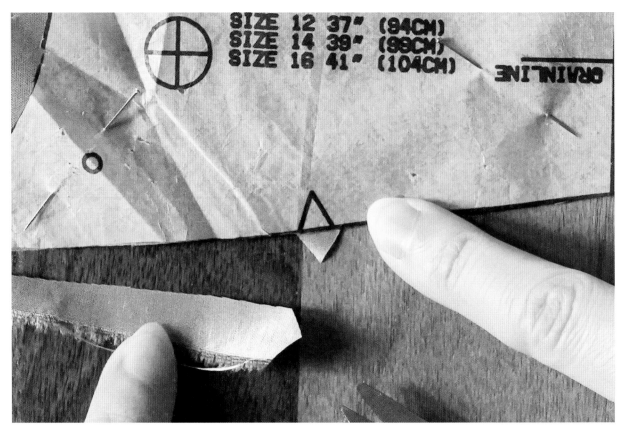

SIZE 12 37" (94CM)
SIZE 14 39" (99CM)
SIZE 16 41" (104CM)

GRAINLINE

A balance mark, or notch, indicated on a pattern and cut onto the material. This will help to align corresponding pattern pieces.

Don't Forget the Balance Marks!

If you're using a predrafted pattern, these will often come with balance marks, or notches, indicated as triangles or dashes at the edge of your pattern piece. These will help you to perfectly match your garment pieces in areas where it may not be clear which edges go together; for example, when attaching sleeves into armscyes, where it may be easy to accidentally rotate the sleeve in the armhole. Sometimes balance marks are placed two or three in a row where these need to be differentiated from another set of marks. Either cutting outward-facing triangles (do not cut into the seam allowance) or marking these points with pencil or thread will help you keep track of exactly where things need to be pieced together.

If you're drafting your own pattern, particularly if you're draping on a dress form, it can be helpful to draw balance marks across panels at crucial points, such as on armscyes, sleeves and bodice panels, so that you may transfer these to your pattern for ease of reference later.

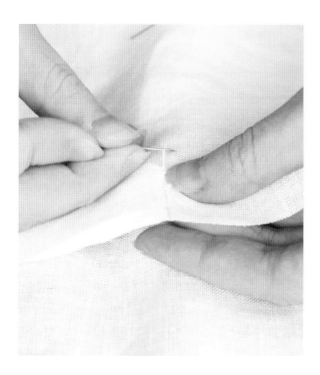

Precision Tip: Drawing Threads

This is a technique that can be used to achieve perfectly on-grain shapes, but can only be used on square and rectangular pattern pieces cut from plain-weave materials. It is far more time-consuming than simply cutting out by eye, but produces shapes that are undeniably and absolutely, perfectly on grain.

At the point of your desired pattern piece, use a pin to gently work a thread free from the weave. Continue pulling this thread all the way along the lengths and widths of your pattern pieces. The threads do often snap, particularly in fabrics made from threads with more loosely twisted fibers, which today is most fabrics. When this happens, simply pick up the end of the thread with the pin and continue pulling it out.

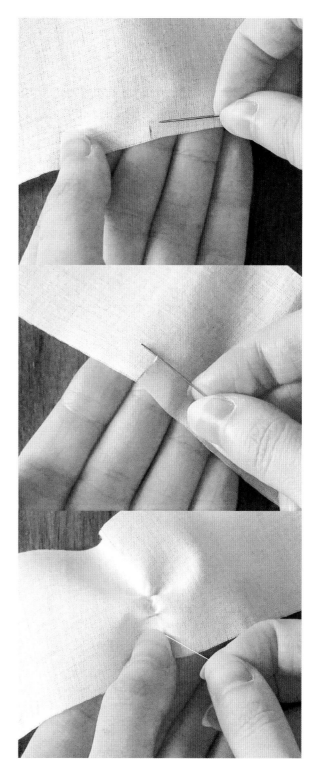

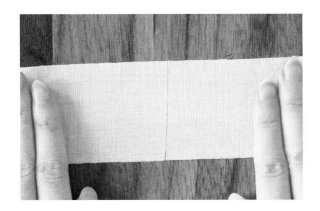

Eventually you will have marked out the square or rectangular shape of your desired pattern piece by means of exposing a small gap in the weave of the material. This provides a perfect line on which you can then go through and cut along to achieve a perfect on-grain cut.

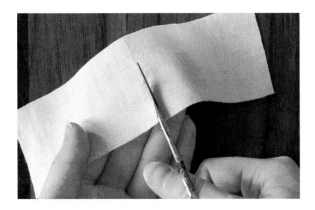

It is also possible, although less precise, simply to attempt to follow a single thread as you cut out straight- or cross-grain edges of your pattern pieces; this compromises the time spent on the thread-drawing portion of the task, although it's not always exact as our eyes don't always follow a single thread perfectly; still, it will produce a more precise cut than not attempting this at all.

Pinning

Pinning your fabric into place before stitching can be helpful in temporarily holding pieces together before they can be properly stitched. There is much heated debate on The Proper Method of Pinning—whether to pin parallel or perpendicularly to your stitching line—although I find that both methods have their benefits and drawbacks worth taking into consideration.

Perpendicular pinning: This method is preferable for machine stitching because the pins can be quickly and easily removed without having to stop every time you reach a pin. This method, however, covers less distance along your seam line, so it will not hold your fabric in position quite as precisely. It is generally not advised to sew over pins with domestic sewing machines, but if you're using an industrial machine (or going *very* slowly and wearing eye protection), perpendicular pins will pass under a needle, whereas parallel pins won't.

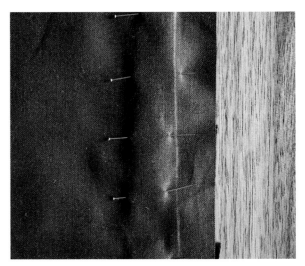

Perpendicular pinning

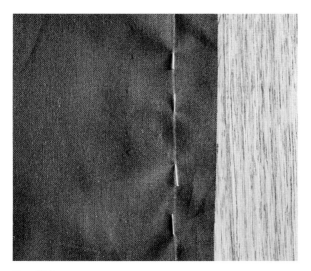

Parallel pinning

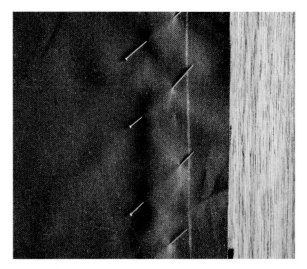

Diagonal pinning

Parallel pinning: This method is capable of holding longer lengths of your stitch line in place, giving you a more precise positioning of your materials. If you're working with a net pattern and have a marked stitching line, this method allows you to perfectly match the stitching lines on both pieces of material along a distance, rather than the single point allowed in perpendicular pinning. This method, however, can make machine sewing rather tedious as you will need to continually stop or slow down to remove the pins as you go. This method takes a bit more time than perpendicular pinning, but is ideal for hand sewing because you won't need to worry about extracting the pins quickly and can benefit from the greater precision.

Diagonal pinning: This is the method I personally prefer to use for machine-sewn projects. It's a nice compromise between occupying a slightly longer distance along the stitch line while also being easy to remove during machine stitching and being quick to put in.

Subtle warp in the material caused by the pins

Remember that placing pins into your material will subtly warp your fabric. This isn't a problem for most simple seams, but this can begin to cause great problems on tasks requiring smoothness and precision, such as when trying to layer two pieces of material smoothly (in linings, for example) or when working with wobbly fabrics, such as charmeuse or organza. To avoid accidentally stitching bubbles into your seam or letting the fabric shift out of place, it is best to pin first, then baste your seam, *then* sew it finally into place.

Piecing Is Period

Fabric was expensive, historically—and in some cases, still is today; but in the days before mechanical weaving when all fabric was produced by hand on manually operated looms, overbuying on expensive yardage was not common practice. Extant garments from many centuries up to the turn of the 20th display unashamed piecing in everything from everyday and work wear to right down the center fronts of elaborately expensive court gowns.[4] Fabric was not only highly valuable—and thus not to be wasted—but was also often woven on smaller looms, resulting in smaller widths; some more elaborate and expensive silks were often around 20 inches (51 cm) in width,[5] meaning that seams had to be placed wherever they had to be placed—sometimes regardless of pattern matching or grain line.

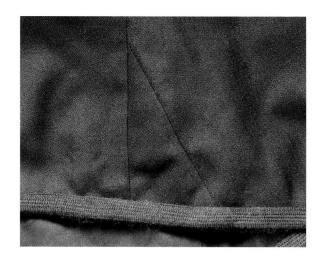

So, if you wish to save on yardage costs and maximize your fabric usage by puzzling your fabric together—or if you've accidentally cut something the wrong way and need to add a corner or an extra panel to a piece—you're in very good company.

Feature: Claudia Vogt

Everywhere I go, people stare at me. It doesn't matter what I wear; they take one look at me, see the wheelchair and make assumptions. Even when not using my wheelchair, if I mention it, people are shocked. "Surely you're not that disabled?" Well, yes; yes I am.

People's idea of what it means to be disabled is so outdated, and with a variable condition like mine, myalgic encephalomyelitis (ME), I simply don't fit the stereotype people have in their head. I constantly have to fight a narrative that other people write for me. If I'm not a tragic victim, I'm an inspiration for "overcoming my disability." But I'm not here for your pity or to make you feel better about yourself. I'm just trying to live my life and clothes have given me a way to rewrite the narrative to reflect the person I really am.

I like my style to be feminine but grown-up and so I turn to the Golden Age of Hollywood for my style inspiration. The styles of the 1930s and '40s celebrate everything people don't expect of a disabled person: high glamour, femininity and, dare I say it, sex appeal? I love to subvert expectations like that. It gives me a feeling of control over my identity when my disability means I have to surrender so much control to others.

I began with simply buying vintage clothes. For me, the thrill of the chase is all part of the fun, but when you have limited means (and energy), you're much more restricted in what you can buy. A lot of my clothes are modern and thrifted but made to look vintage. I trained and worked as a costumier, and so I have a lot of experience making modern items do for an historical style. You can get great results from easy switches like changing the buttons or adding a lace trim. Little projects like that are a great place to start if you're intimidated by bigger projects, or are simply short on time and energy.

Despite my health, I still make my own clothes from scratch. It's an important creative outlet for me and it gives me even more control over my self-expression. Over the years I've come up with lots of little hacks that mean I can keep on sewing even when I'm very sick. I use some adaptive equipment, but mostly I just go at my own pace and remember to take lots of breaks. And if I'm too sick to sew, I knit from bed! My goal is not to make things quickly, but to make them in a way that is right for me. And that is true of the finished garment as well as the process.

I truly believe that every time we get dressed, we make an artistic statement about the person we are, or rather the person we want others to see. When people stare at me, I want them to see more than a wheelchair user. I want them to see who I am.

—Claudia Vogt (she/her)

The
Stitches

With the ready availability of fast and powerful electric sewing machines today, we've generally reserved hand sewing for the rare, tedious tasks that machines can't do. Unfortunately, this means that when—or *if*—we learn to hand sew, we often do so with appropriate delicacy—not with the level of strength required to produce long-lasting, hard-wearing garments.

Sewing That Stands the Test of Time

Although 19th-century sewing may look delicate in appearance, these clothes were built to last. The sewing machine was still new enough in the second part of the century that garment construction wasn't yet solely reliant on machine stitching, and much of the construction work—particularly on homemade garments—was still done by hand. In fact, most household sewing guides you'll read up until the turn of the 20th century hardly mention machine sewing at all. Prior to the introduction of electric industrial machinery that facilitates mass-manufacture processes today, the garment construction process took a little bit more time, and thus, the 21st-century concept of a $10 fast fashion blouse wasn't a reality for shoppers in the 19th century. The average person's wardrobe was fairly limited,[6] as buying new clothes every month was neither practical nor necessary for most people. Strength in hand sewing and skill in mending was therefore essential to ensuring that clothes stood the test of time—and that the buyer got their money's worth.

In this chapter, we'll go through some essential stitching techniques that you can use to make entire new garments—or just to mend or reinforce the ones you already have.

But first, let's talk about the tools we need to make that happen.

There are a few I've found more essential to actually making stitches, and a few that are just nice to have.

Essential Tools

Needles

Highly essential for sewing things. I like to keep an assortment of lengths and thicknesses at hand to use in accordance with the material I'm working with. In general, my go-to needle is a #10 sharp (L)—fairly small and slim, as you'll be able to more naturally work smaller stitches with a smaller and thinner needle. Thicker fabrics, such as heavy wools, however, may require a longer needle as the thickness of the material will take up more needle length per stitch. Basting is also best done with a longer needle, as more space can be covered per stitch, and it is also helpful to have a big tapestry needle (R) on hand for threading ribbon or cord through eyelets as well as inserting cording into channels. Thick needles should be used with caution, as they can leave visible holes in delicate silks, but can also be difficult to pass through materials with a tight weave. Slimmer needles, though more prone to bending against tougher jobs, will pass through a tighter weave more easily—so sometimes the sacrifice is worth it.

Thread

Also highly essential for actually sewing things. Regular polyester thread is the most widely used due to its availability, strength, machine compatibility and low cost. There are also natural-fiber thread options for those working in historical or eco-friendly practices, but not all of these will be compatible with electric sewing machines. Linen threads, for example, tend to be unceremoniously consumed by electric machines, but work very well in hand sewing. Linen threads—and later in the 19th century, cotton threads—were used so frequently that the word *cotton* was often used synonymously with *thread* in contemporary sewing guides. Silk thread was and still is also commonly used, although due to its cost was mostly reserved for visible places on garments made from silk fabrics.

Silk thread is the strongest of the natural-fiber threads, so it was used in places that required strength, for example, in hard-wearing places, such as eyelets or buttonholes. Linen thread was extremely prevalent in the 18th and earlier centuries due to its wide availability and low cost. However, this is not so easy to source today and, although cotton and silk threads are easy enough to come by, linen thread often needs to be purchased from specialty suppliers catering to the historical reenactment or weaving market. Linen thread will need to be coated with beeswax before use to smooth the rough fibers, which will otherwise catch in the fabric and weaken the thread. It is usual to then wrap the coated thread in paper and press with an iron to allow the wax to be absorbed by the thread.

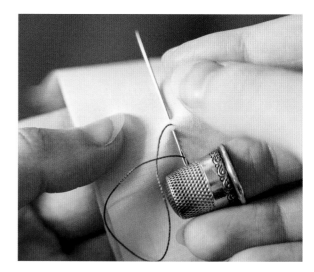

Wax

If you're planning to use linen thread, you'll need a block of beeswax for smoothing the linen fibers before use. Waxing any type of thread can be useful for additional strength or to prevent the thread from twisting as you sew.

Thimble

Thimbles are extraordinarily essential creatures, although they do take some getting used to initially. If you're doing any amount of prolonged hand sewing, you will need to preserve the state of your fingers. Painful fingers means slower sewing, so getting acclimated to using a thimble as soon as possible will speed up your sewing in the long run.

The thimble is worn on the middle finger of your dominant hand, which is the finger used to push the needle through the material. Today, they're available in hard form (plastic or metal) or in soft leather.

Soft thimbles are easiest to get used to and are very easy to make yourself: Simply trace the tip of your middle finger down to the first joint onto two scraps of leather, then whipstitch (page 63) the two halves together with some strong thread. These don't tend to last as long as hard thimbles.

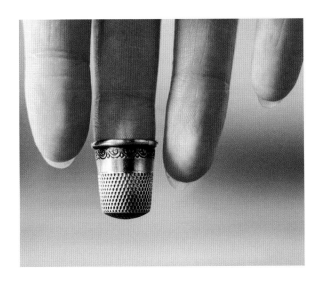

Hard thimbles are made either in the dressmaker's style with the closed top, or the tailor's style with the open top. Your stitching style, and whether you naturally use the top or the side of the thimble to push the needle (or whether you have long fingernails), will dictate which style is most suitable to your sewing needs.

Hard thimbles are sized and must be properly fit for efficient use; a thimble that continually falls off isn't practical for efficient use. To test the fit of your thimble, place it on your middle finger. It should fit snugly, and should not slip off when you turn your hand fingers-side down.

Tip:

If you have a metal thimble that is just slightly too big, try gently squishing it with a pair of pliers.

Many thimbles that survive from past centuries show evidence of this hack having been employed.

Embroidery Snips

A small pair of scissors for clipping threads.

Pins

Steel-headed straight pins are well documented throughout history, but the glass- or plastic-headed pins of today will do just as well. I find longer pins to be more useful than shorter pins, which will not be as efficient: size 17 (1¹⁄₁₆ inches [27 mm]) or size 20 (1½ inches [32 mm]) should be perfect for most sewing purposes. Be sure that your pins aren't too thick (0.6 mm or less) or they will require more force to pass through fabric and will leave visible holes. You may want to find very fine pins (0.4 to 0.5 mm) for working with dense, tightly woven fabrics, but be careful with these—they will be prone to bending easily.

Tape Measure

For taking measurements. Flexible fiberglass tape measures are usually best, as some cloth tape measures can stretch over time and distort your measurements. It's a good idea in general to regularly check your flexible tape measures against a solid wooden or metal ruler to ensure that your measures are consistent. Flexible measures should not generally be used for precise measurements: Solid measures such as those made from wood, metal or plastic quilting rulers are better for the more precision-based tasks, such as pattern drafting, but flexible measures are necessary for such tasks as measuring the body. Avoid storing tape measures in a tight roll, as this can stretch the outer layers. It is also important to measure the first and last inch or centimeter before using: Sometimes a metal reinforcement is added to the front and back of the tape, and it may not measure the full increment. When using my flexible measure, I always treat the second inch as the first inch, since the first is about ⅛ inch (3 mm) short of a full inch.

A note from history: Long before the flexible tape measure was introduced, body measurements were taken using long, thin strips of paper with each measurement noted directly on the paper strip: waist circumference, arm length and so on—no numbers needed. This made such tasks as halving or quartering measurements (in pattern drafting, for example) extremely easy: Simply fold the measure and transfer that distance directly onto the paper without ever having to glance at fractions. This technique can be used if you don't feel like buying a tape measure, or if you prefer to work without the math involved in converting measurement systems or working with numbers in general. When using this system, it is usually helpful to work with two separate strips: one to note lengths (inseam, outseam, shoulder-to-wrist, etc.) and one to note circumferences (waist, hips, chest, etc.) as your measure can get a bit crowded if you're taking full body measures on a single strip.

Marking Supplies

For marking out pattern pieces—especially if you're working with patterns that don't include seam allowance, or that need darts or tucks marked onto the fabric. These can include, according to your preference: pencil (both colored tailor's pencils or standard graphite) or charcoal for lighter materials, or tailor's chalk for darker materials. If using a block of chalk to mark, always ensure that the marking edges of this are kept sharp to produce precise lines. Dedicated sharpening tools are available, but this can just as easily be done with a knife or scissor blade. Modern disappearing and heat-sensitive inks, such as FriXion pens, can also be useful.

Iron

Neatly pressed seams make all the difference. Be sure to set to the correct temperature for your fabric.

Shears

It's nice to have a separate pair of fabric shears for cutting out material. If you've ever tried to cut cloth with your average household scissors, you may already understand why; paper, boxes, packaging and general household cutting tasks are very abrasive on scissor blades and can dull them quickly. To avoid frayed or choppy cutting on your nice garment pieces, it's best to have a dedicated pair of fabric shears that are to be used for fabric and nothing else. Shears can be purchased in right- or left-handed configurations, or with spring-loading to ease cutting action for those with limited hand movement.

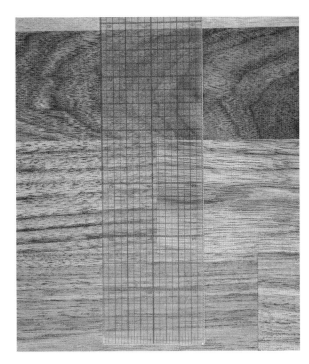

Nice-to-Have Tools

Seam Ripper

We all mess up and need to unpick things sometimes, but a seam ripper isn't a tool I reach for very often. Although these are relatively inexpensive to obtain and it can be nice to have a dedicated item to use specifically for unpicking purposes, more often than not I just clip my erroneous threads with a small pair of embroidery scissors instead.

Plastic Quilter's Ruler

For measuring and pattern drafting.

French Curve

For drawing the curved bits when drafting patterns.

Tailor's Ham

A curved cushion intended to assist with pressing curved bits of a garment. These are also great to use as an anchor for pinning your hand sewing into so that you have some tension to pull against while you sew. It makes the work go much quicker and produces much neater seams.

Awl

This can be useful for opening up holes in the weave of material without splitting the threads, which can then be finished off into eyelets.

The nice-to-have possibilities are endless, with fun new gadgets popping up regularly, from binding makers to eyelet-spacing rulers to magnetic pincushions. While these aren't essential to the fundamental process of making a garment, they can certainly make your process a bit easier (or at least a bit more fun) if you feel like treating yourself.

Starting and Finishing the Thread

If using linen thread, be sure to run the length over a block of beeswax a few times before threading it through the needle so that the fibers are smoothed and strengthened.

Thread Single

To thread *single*, the needle is threaded and the tail of the thread left loose so that it may feed back through the eye as you stitch. This allows you to use more thread at a time without the thread being so long that it tangles and knots while you stitch. The length of thread from the eye of the needle to the cut end should be approximately the length of your forearm[7] for maximum speed and efficiency, and the tail should not exceed the length of the main thread. You'll spend far less time knotting off and restarting new threads than you will continually untangling, untwisting and deknotting a thread that is too long.

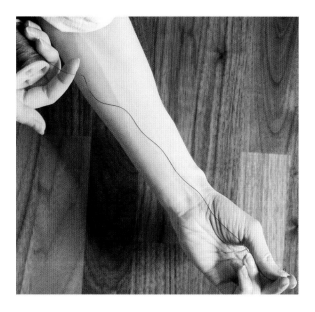

The needle is not tied to the thread but is left free to slide along the length of the thread, so the additional length of the tail can be shifted as the length of the thread shortens.

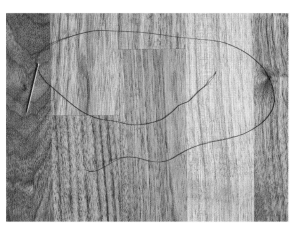

Thread Double

You may in some cases wish to thread *double* when you need to cover greater amounts of space with a stitch, such as in eyelet hole or buttonhole making, or if extra strength is needed in a stitch. This form of threading is not as commonly used as single threading. In this case, the thread is passed through the eye of the needle and then the two ends of the tail are matched up, with the needle resting in the crook of the thread at the halfway point. You may knot the two ends together if you wish, although it is just as efficient (and less

conspicuous) to anchor these thread ends into the fabric when beginning in the same manner as with single threading.

If you're sewing two pieces of fabric together and the space between the layers won't be seen, you can bury the end of the thread between these two layers for a neat start. This ability to hide thread tails within the layers of fabric is a primary reason that knotting the end of your thread is not desirable, as in this case, the tails of the thread will always be exposed.

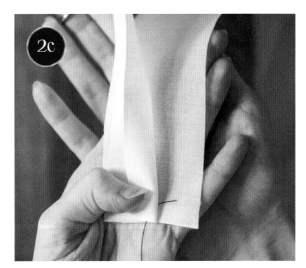

1. Insert the threaded needle a small distance away from your intended starting point so that it only pierces the uppermost layer of fabric but does not go through both layers.

2. Travel a small distance (perhaps an inch or two [2.5 to 5 cm]) until you reach your starting point, then bring the needle back up, drawing the thread so that the end disappears between the layers but is not pulled through the exit point.

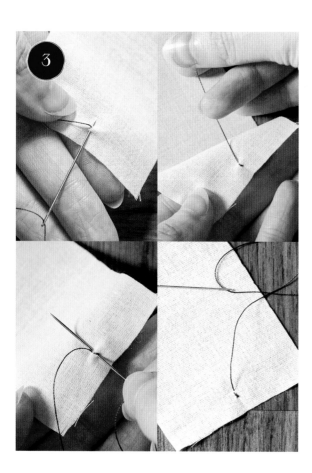

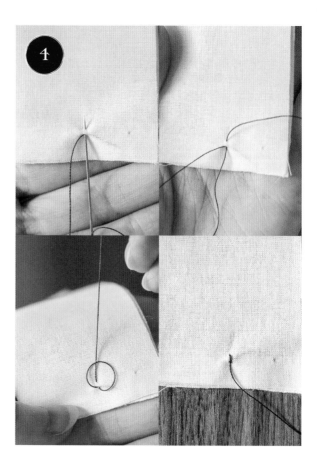

3. From the exit point, take several small backstitches (page 59) in place, the size you intend the rest of your stitches to be.

4. For additional security, you may opt to pass the needle through the loop of the stitch before pulling it through, to create a small knot. This tightens the hold of the thread but also creates a more noticeable bulk in the seam.

5. After finishing your seam, the process of starting the thread is repeated in reverse to finish it securely. Once again, this can be done either with a knot or with several stationary backstitches.

The needle is passed back through the top layer of material and out a small distance away from the seam, then the excess thread is clipped away.

Stitches to Know

Running Stitch

This is the simplest stitch, and though not the strongest option, running stitching is best for speed. For this reason, it's used for longer seams that don't need to take significant strain, such as long skirt seams or the side seams of a loose garment. Running stitching is also often used in darning (page 176) and for basting (page 56).

This stitch is done by taking up and passing over regular numbers of threads in the weave of the fabric in a continuous line.

A smaller stitch length (12 or fewer stitches per inch [2.5 cm]) will produce a stronger seam, whereas a longer stitch length (greater than 12 stitches per inch [2.5 cm]) will be looser but easier to remove, so this latter is more desirable for basting.

The number of threads taken up and passed over is simply a way of monitoring your stitching so that you can easily correct yourself should you find the stitches growing too big or too small, but it's not necessary to sit and count threads with a magnifier between each stitch.[8] As much as I'm sure we all love precise sewing, it's probably not worth letting the sewing get in the way of having a nice new garment to wear.

Suggested Materials

Needle

Thread

Wax (if desired)

Thimble

Thread snips

Steps

1. After beginning your thread securely according to the previous instructions on starting your thread (pages 49 and 50), proceed to take up and pass over your desired number of threads at regular intervals.

2. Repeat this process to produce an even line of stitching.

Speed tip:

Once you've got the hang of this stitch, you can stop taking each stitch individually and start loading your needle with several stitches at a time before pulling it through. Just be sure to smooth the material after pulling the needle—a thread pulled too tightly will cause the fabric to pucker, and a thread left too loose will leave room for it to snag.

Basting

Basting refers to any stitch done as a temporary means of tacking two or more pieces of material together so that they lie securely and flat, avoiding the subtle rippling that can be caused by the use of pins. Most often basting is done with a long running stitch with the goal of speed over security, as the stitch will be removed before the garment is ready to wear. This stitch is best done with a long needle for extra speed, and the ends of the stitch are not anchored off at the end, for ease of removal.

Suggested Materials

A long needle

Thread

Thimble

Thread snips

Steps

1. Running stitch basting is most often used to hold seams or other linear stretches of a garment together temporarily. See the section on pad stitching (page 69) for an alternative basting technique to secure wide areas of material to one another.

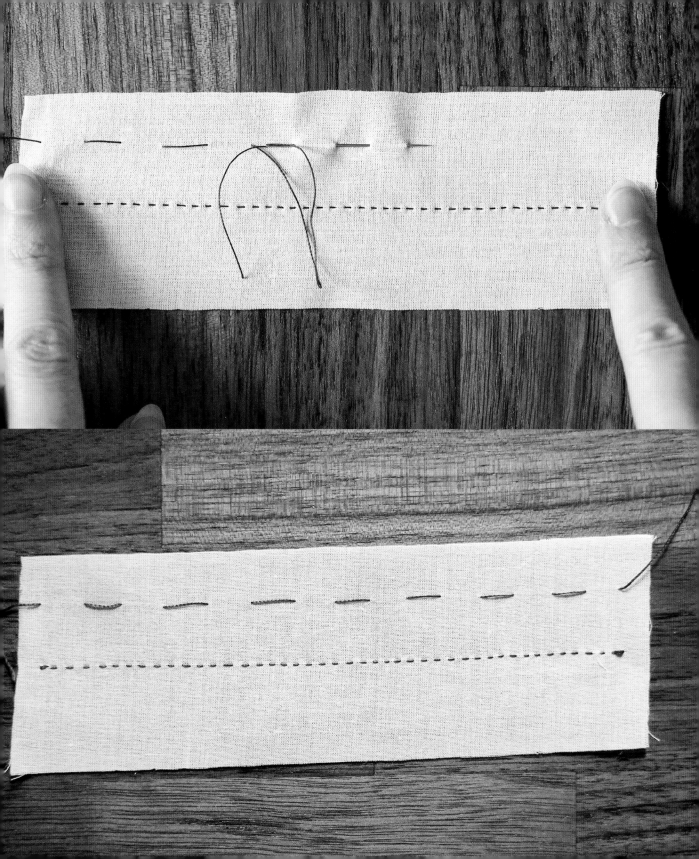

Backstitch

Backstitching is one of the strongest hand stitches and is best used for seams that need to take significant strain. Sleeves, gussets (page 154) and armscyes, as well as tight bodice seams will all do best with a strong backstitch. Backstitching was so common by the late 19th century that some sewing guides call this simply "stitching," with "backstitch" referring to what we would today specify as a "half backstitch."[9]

In a perfect world, we would be able to use backstitches on everything, so as to have perfectly strong seams on all portions of a garment, but unfortunately due to the back-and-forth nature of the working process, these seams take about twice as long to complete as a simple running stitch and so are often sacrificed in favor of faster methods.

Suggested Materials

Needle

Thread

Wax (if desired)

Thimble

Thread snips

Steps

1. A backstitch is done by inserting the needle backward to meet the previous stitch before passing the needle under and exiting a small ways ahead of the current stitch.

2. To avoid splitting the previous thread with your needle when traveling backward, as this will weaken the thread, the needle should be inserted next to the thread in the previous stitch rather than through the thread. This will cause the wrong side of the stitch to appear as a series of slanted lines.

Wrong side of a backstitch　　*A thread that has been split*

3. Once again, the length of stitches is up to you and may best be determined by the thickness of your material, but for proportional reference, the needle will be traveling backward two threads of the fabric weave to meet the last stitch, then forward four threads to end up two threads ahead of the current stitch.

4. This process is repeated, ensuring that the thread is pulled taut for each stitch.

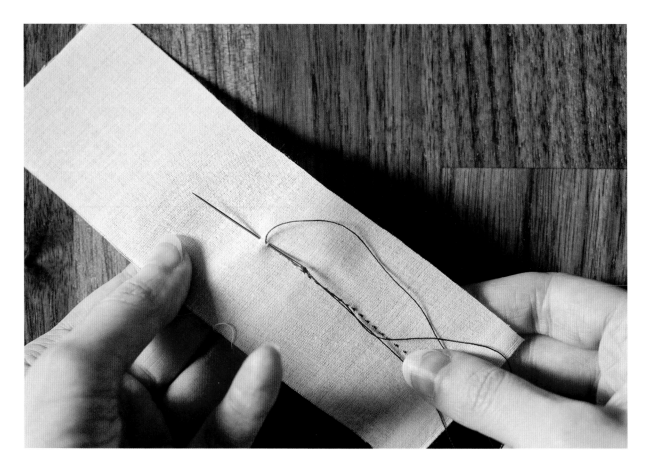

Half Backstitch

If strength is still desired but some compromise must be made on the time spent sewing, a half backstitch (also known as a spaced backstitch) is a great alternative.

This is done by inserting the needle only halfway back between the exit point of the thread and the position of the previous stitch, slightly lessening the distance that the needle will need to travel. As this still requires an element of backward travel for every forward movement, it is still slightly slower than an ordinary running stitch but is similar in strength to a full backstitch.

Right side of half
backstitch

Wrong side of half
backstitch

A single backstitch taken after every two running stitches

Two consecutive running stitches

Combination Stitch

Alternatively, if more speed is required in sewing without forfeiting all the strength of the backstitch, a combination stitch (also known as a running backstitch) may be used.

This is a combination between a running stitch and a backstitch, in which two running stitches are taken forward for every one backstitch. [10]

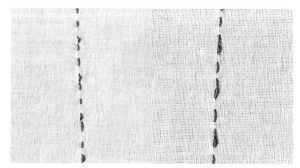

Combination stitch right side   *Combination stitch wrong side*

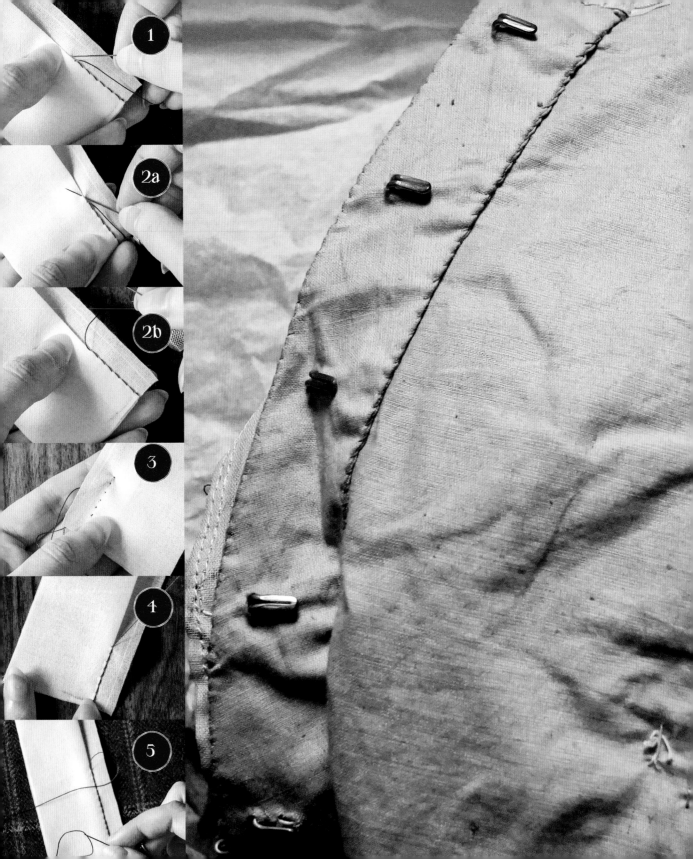

Whipstitch

Whipstitching, otherwise known as felling or hem stitching, is used to secure the edge of one material onto the base of another, such as when hemming (page 90), finishing seams (page 75), overcasting (page 79) or attaching trims to garments.

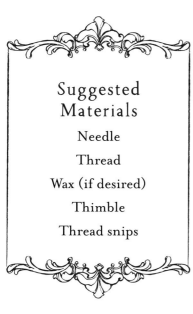

Suggested Materials

Needle

Thread

Wax (if desired)

Thimble

Thread snips

Steps

1. Begin on the base layer, inserting the needle just next to the edge of the top material.

2. Bring the needle diagonally up, so that the edge of the second material is caught. Ideally only the very edge—approximately one or two threads—of this upper fabric is caught so that as little of the felling stitch sits on top of the fabric as possible and the thread buries itself into the space of the fold.

3. The amount of fabric taken up by the needle should be as minimal as possible, as this stitch may show through to the right side of a garment (such as in felling seam allowances or in hemming).

4. Proceed a little ways down the material to take the next stitch. The distance taken is up to you, but after determining the distance at this stage, it should be repeated for the remainder of the seam to ensure neat, regular stitches. A longer distance will make for a faster process and fewer stitches showing through to the other side, but a less secure seam; a smaller distance is more secure but slower, and a greater number of stitches will be visible if this is to show through to the outside of the garment.

5. A finished whipstitch appears as a series of long stitches on the working side and small dashes on the underside.

(continued)

Left: Inside a c. 1860s evening bodice featuring a hook-facing panel felled to the bodice lining

Pin your seam to a tailor's ham or firm cushion.

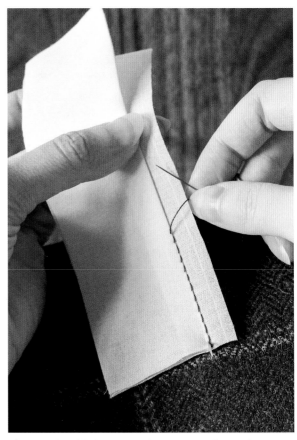

The pin should slant away from you so that it does not come loose when you pull against it.

Whipstitch (Continued)

Speed tip:

Once you've done about ½ to 1 inch (1.3 to 2.5 cm) of the seam, you can pin the nearer end to a tailor's ham, firm cushion or heavy fold of fabric (wool or felt work best) so that you can pull against this for tension. Place the pin right at the base of the seam so that the tension point is centered along the line you're working, and make sure that the pin is slanted into the cushion away from you so that you don't pull it out as you work. Tensioning your work in this way will allow you to achieve neater stitches more quickly, and using a pin to achieve this tension instead of your nondominant hand will save you lots of pain and cramping in the long run.

1. *Unwanted twist in your thread*

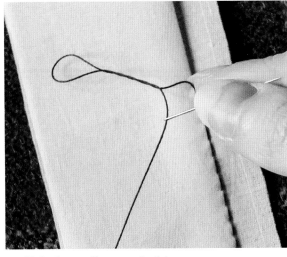

2. *Slide the needle up to the fabric*

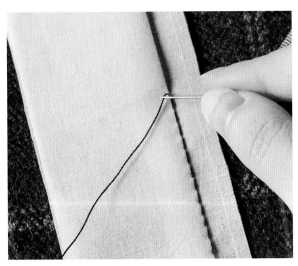

3. *Allow the thread to untwist itself*

4. *Continue stitching as normal*

Caution:

Unlike the previous stitches, the thread in a whipstitch travels in a corkscrew rather than a linear back-and-forward path, so it will develop a twist every couple of inches; unaddressed, this will cause your thread to knot itself as you pull it through, slowing down your stitching pace.

Untwisting the thread is very quick and easy:

Simply slide the needle all the way up the thread so that it meets the fabric, allow the thread to naturally untwist itself, then slide the needle back along the thread so that you have adequate working length once again.

Herringbone Stitch

This stitch (also known as cross or catch stitch) was rare in dressmaking before the 20th century. It was used primarily in securing down fabric edges and in attaching bones into bodices or jackets by the later 19th century. Like the backstitch, the herringbone stitch travels both forward and backward, so it maintains a relatively firm hold; but due to the long distances of traveled thread between stitches, which are left exposed, this stitch is more likely to be caught and pulled. So, while it is relatively quick and aesthetically pleasing, do be careful not to use it on sections of a garment that have the potential to come in contact with anything that may catch the stitching, such as an unlined maxi-skirt hem that may be caught by the heel of a shoe.

The herringbone stitch is particularly useful in hemming (page 90) and attaching bones or stays into bodices or collars. It is worked laterally and in the opposite direction of the needle; so if you are right-handed and pointing the needle to the left, the stitch will be worked from left to right; if you are left-handed and pointing the needle to the right, you will be traveling from right to left.

Suggested
Materials

Needle

Thread

Wax (if desired)

Thimble

Thread snips

Steps

This demonstration is worked right-handed, from left to right. This stitch may show through to the right side of the material, so stitches should be as small as the thickness of your material will allow.

1. Begin with a small backstitch at the appropriate starting point, according to your dominant hand. It is best to begin your thread on the thicker side of the fabric so that a knot may be buried between the layers of material (see instructions for starting and finishing the thread [page 49]).

2. This next stitch will determine the distance vertically and horizontally that you will need to repeat so as to produce evenly crossed stitches. It doesn't matter how large or small these distances are, as long as they're repeated regularly along the remainder of the seam. This stitch is taken on the thin side of the material, a small distance across in the opposite direction from which your needle is pointing.

3. Now that you have determined the distances to travel, repeat these distances by moving upward to the level of the first stitch, and the same distance farther across, taking another stitch at this point.

4. Continue along the length of the material as desired. The final stitch should produce a neat row of crossing stitches.

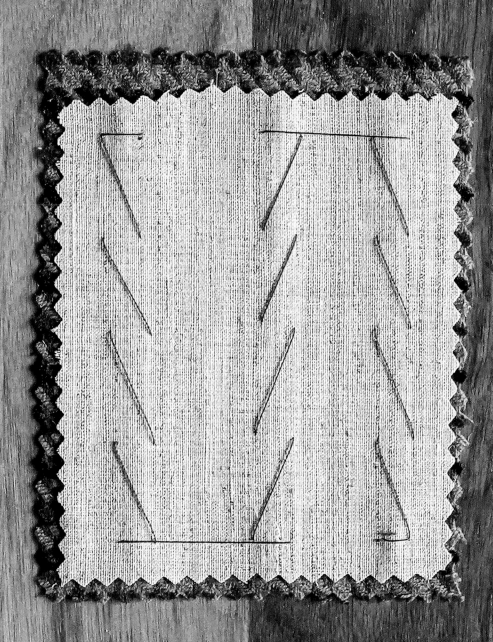

Pad Stitching

How do you give a fabric structure, or make it sit evenly round a curve? How do you get two layers of slippery satin or organza to behave while you stitch, so you don't end up with a bubbled mess?

While pad stitching isn't a fundamental structural seam, I like to think of it as the secret weapon of stitches: the way to secure two layers of fabric neatly together, whether temporarily until they're sewn into proper position, or whether in training the layers to go around a curve, preemptively manipulating them into their three-dimensional shape. Pad stitching is intended to be a permanent, structural layer of stitching and is common in tailoring, where collars must be shaped with an interlining to curve around the neck without bubbling or where jacket fronts must be curved smoothly across the chest. But this same technique can also be used on a larger scale to temporarily secure two layers of fabric together, in which case it is known as basting.

This stitch is useful to temporarily hold large layers of material together so that they don't bubble or warp when you go to stitch them. For example, if you want to add a stiffening layer to a wobbly material, pad stitching can help control that wobbly layer by connecting it to the stiff layer exactly where you want it to go so that it won't sneak around before you go to stitch it. Pad stitching can also help to add shape to areas like collars, or to help the lapels of a jacket roll back smoothly; effectively, this stitch helps preemptively tell the fabric how to behave before it's made up into a garment. The stitches are worked vertically, usually on two fabrics layered together; work is usually done from the interlining side so that the stitch will show through as minimally as possible from the right side.

The stitch in this demonstration would likely be a basting stitch due to the stitch size and length done for clarity, and would be meant to hold two or more layers of material temporarily together to be removed later. Generally for permanent pad stitching, the stitch taken up by the needle is much smaller (roughly ¼ inch [6 mm]) so that as little of the thread as possible is seen from the fabric side of the material.

Suggested Materials

Needle

Thread

Wax (if desired)

Thimble

Thread snips

Tip:

To ensure that the layers of material remain in position and don't shift while the basting is put in, work the first row of pad stitching from the center of the panel and out to one side, then from the center and out to the other so that the fabric remains correctly positioned, and any excess width is pushed off to the edge of the panel instead of pushed into bubbles in the center.

(continued)

Pad Stitching (Continued)

Steps

1. Begin by taking a single backstitch at the top of the material to secure the thread. The scale of your pad stitching will depend on the project, whether the stitch is to be a basting stitch or a structural stitch, as well as how quickly you want to finish.

2. The distance traveled vertically will depend on whether your stitch is to be a temporary basting stitch or a permanent structural stitch; temporary stitches should be long (anywhere from 1 to 4 inches [2.5 to 10 cm] depending on the expanse of material to be covered), as they will be easier to remove later; permanent stitches should be much shorter (approximately ¼ to ½ inch [6 mm to 1.3 cm]) as more frequent stitching will allow you to work more shape into the garment. The needle for this second stitch should be inserted directly below the entry point of the stitch above, creating a diagonal thread that travels from the exit point of the last stitch to the entry point of the new one.

3. Repeat this process down the length of your material, keeping your horizontal entry and exit points aligned with one thread in the fabric to ensure a perfectly straight row of stitches. This is more important in permanent stitching than in basting; precise alignment is not strictly necessary in basting. If the fabric doesn't have a straight grain line for you to follow—or you're deliberately working off grain—you can preemptively draw some guidelines onto the interlining of the fabric at your desired width so that you can ensure that you're working in straight rows.

4. When you reach the bottom, carry over a small distance laterally, leaving a long horizontal thread.

5. Take another horizontal stitch, the same size as the stitches taken in the previous column.

6. This time, traveling upward, take another stitch above according to the distances taken in the previous column. The stitches will begin to form a chevron pattern.

7. As the rows are worked, it's important to hold the material in the shape you wish the final garment to take. Geometry dictates that, in curved shapes, the innermost curve has a slightly smaller surface area than the outer curve, so you'll need to mold your fabric into this position if it's not meant to sit absolutely flat. For example, on a collar piece that is meant to curve around the neck, or a lapel that is meant to roll back onto the body, the stitches should be worked with the layers of fabric wrapped around a finger to obtain that tight or gently curved shape.

8. If using a pad stitch for basting, be sure that your fabrics are in their intended position before tacking the layers into place, as this will ensure your fabric edges won't be in undesirable positions before you've stitched the seams together.

9. The completed pad stitching area will appear as a series of columns with stitches slanting in alternating directions to form a chevron pattern, and as columns of small horizontal dashes on the underside. In permanent pad stitching, this underside may be the outside of your garment, which is why pad stitching should be worked from the "wrong" or inner side of a garment, and the stitches taken up by the needle should be as small as possible.

Feature: Yang Cheon Shik

The depth of fulfillment that comes from wearing garments that you have made yourself, moreover, traditional garments that your ancestors have worn for centuries, simply cannot be understated. 안 녕 하 세 요 ! Annyeong-haseyo! (Hello!) My name is Cheon Shik Yang and I am a transracial Korean adoptee. I make and wear hanbok (the traditional dress of Korea) every day.

Born in Korea, I was adopted into a white family in the United States, given a Western name and grew up with little to no connectivity to my heritage, traditions and people. While I was growing up, identity and connectivity to Korean culture were driving points for me—wondering what and where I had come from, in terms of a rich culture and centuries of history and tradition not taught in schools. As I grew to embrace my identity, learning Korean, studying any and all texts and sources to know the things lost by way of adoption, I finally bought my first set of hanbok and the feeling was indescribable. Usually reserved for holidays and special occasions, hanbok is worn by very few on a daily basis, though a goodly number of Korean designers are working to modernize and bring forth a new wave of daily wear hanbok.

As someone who has always been crafty and "on a budget," I knew some sewing basics and would alter, dye or embroider preexisting garments to make my own unique wardrobe and extend textile usage. As I dove into the historical dress community, I found the inspiration to make my own hanbok in an effort of both sustainability against fast fashion and to dig deeper into the techniques and processes of chimseon, traditional Korean sewing. Studying garments and patterns used for hundreds of years, the histories surrounding each garment and its original use, as well as the sourcing of fabric all give me a greater understanding of my history, my people and myself.

I tend to stay within the Joseon Dynasty (1392–1897) and Korean Empire (1897–1910) in terms of my inspirational time period, Joseon being the period from which hanbok as we visually know it today comes from. I try to vary my wardrobe with a comfortable mix of more historically inspired pieces, such as the wide-sleeved dopo outer robe to modern interpretations, such as a shortened, slimmed-down version of a pleated military garment called a cheollik.

As I've gone about my life dressed in full hanbok, though not without its own special set of difficulties in social interaction, I've been able to meet and get to know the amazing Korean and AAPI community I've always dreamed of. Understandably, dressing as unapologetically Korean as I do is not the comfort level for most people, but I cannot fully express the strength and grounding that comes from embracing one's own heritage, whether visually viewed outward as I do or internally as a stronger sense of self. By layering myself in history, tradition and culture, I have found a new path that I could not be prouder to be on.

—양천식

Yang Cheon Shik (he/him)

Applications

Finishing the Edges

Fabrics that are woven (i.e., not felted wools, solid materials such as leather or PVC or some knits such as cotton jersey) will be prone to unraveling if the edges are left raw and unfinished after a seam is stitched or an edge cut. Over time, this can deteriorate your garment as these threads can loosen themselves and eventually dissolve your seam. While historically many edges of tightly woven materials were left raw with no damaging effect, hand-woven materials produced in the past tended to be more tightly woven than the majority of fabrics produced today, which are now machine-woven with much looser weaves and are therefore more prone to fraying. This isn't to say that all fabrics today are ubiquitously prone to fraying. The edges of tightly woven 100 percent wools are often safe to leave raw as these edges will felt over time, and some fine cottons and silks are still tightly woven enough to get away with the occasional raw edge. You can determine whether a fabric will be stable enough to be left raw by rubbing the edge and assessing how badly the fabric frays. A fabric that comes off in strands will likely need to be finished, whereas those that require substantial aggravation before fraying will likely be fine raw.

Overlockers (also known as sergers, machines designed to finish fabrics by trimming and working multiple threads to bind off the raw edges) are more common, both domestically and industrially, so the finishing of raw edges is not as laborious a process as it sometimes was historically. In the absence of an overlocking machine, however, it is still possible to finish edges with strength and neatness to ensure longevity in your seams, each varying in degrees of speed and durability.

A Note on Period Imperfection

Don't let a fear of imperfect stitches stop you from getting your hands on some sewing.

For all the meticulous stitching practice preached by the sewing manuals of the late 19th century, for all proclamations of which methods are "good" or "bad" practice, extant garments reveal that there was a clear difference between ideal sewing practices and the reality: corners that were cut and shortcuts taken for time or impatience. Wonky hand and machine stitching can be seen in the work of home sewers who just wanted a garment to be wearably Good Enough. Manufacturers were often racing against the clock to maximize their product sales; and yes, even in Worth gowns—Victorian haute couture—there's a bit of imperfection in all manner of garments.

Pinking

Perhaps the simplest and fastest way to finish an edge is by using a set of pinking shears to cut a serrated pattern into the raw edge of the seam. Staggering the length of the raw ends of the threads will prevent the threads from coming loose in long strands that catch and pull additional threads loose.

Pinking works best on stiff silks such as taffeta, fine cottons and tightly woven wools that will felt. It is not recommended for looser weaves, as loosely woven threads may still come undone despite the pinked edge.

Steps

1. Using a pair of pinking shears, carefully cut along your raw edge so that all frayed edges are cut away and you are left with a neat, even scalloped or serrated edge.

Suggested
Materials

Pinking shears

Right: Pinking used to finish the seam allowances of this bodice lining, c. 1898

1a

1b

1c

Overcasting

Overcasting, like pinking, is another fast but relatively less secure way of finishing edges, wherein a large whipstitch is worked over the edge of the material to bind the exposed threads into place and prevent them from working loose. It was a highly common edge finishing method in the 19th century and is employed on most materials, especially on long skirt seams where speed is preferred, or on single-layer bodices where a turn-and-fell finish would be visible from the right side of the garment.

Overcasting is a great choice for most fabric types with a medium to tight weave, but is not effective on very loosely woven fabrics with a high tendency for fraying.

Suggested
Materials

Needle

Thread

Thimble

Thread snips

Steps

1. Work a series of whipstitches a fair way deep into the seam allowance so that the stitch anchors the fabric yarns securely rather than pulling them out. The depth of the stitch should be slightly varied so that strain is not placed along one single yarn in the weave of the fabric. The distance between stitches may be varied according to the maker's discretion, with more frequent stitches producing a more secure finish and longer stitches saving on time. A ¼ inch to ½ inch (6 mm to 12 mm) stitch length is often ideal.

2. When stitching, ensure that the thread is pulled tightly enough so that it is not so loose as to snag but is not so tight as to warp the edge of the seam allowance.

Left: Overcasting used to finish the seam allowances of a c. 1880s bodice

Binding

Binding can be a good choice of finish when working with heavier fabrics or thick garment edges, such as the edges of stays, tie-on pockets and some seam allowances. To achieve this, a strip of fabric or thin ribbon is folded around the raw edge to cover the exposed edges.

Binding strips today are generally cut on the bias so that they are easier to stretch around curved portions of garments without bubbling, but historically bindings were most commonly straight-of-grain, as cutting bias strips across the fabric was undesirably wasteful of precious and expensive material. It is possible to bind edges—even curved edges—neatly with either grain, but when using straight-of-grain binding strips, it is essential to keep these as narrow as the thickness of your material will allow—usually no greater than ½ inch (12 mm).

Suggested Materials

Needle

Thread

Wax (if desired)

Thimble

Scissors

Premade binding if you
will not be cutting
your own

Steps

1. To obtain binding strips, you may wish to cut strips from a chosen material to any width desired (keeping in mind that the binding will need to fold in half to encase the raw edge, and if raw edges are involved, you will require further seam allowance for turning under). Alternatively, strips of ribbon or tape may be used. If you have cut your own binding from a fabric, resulting in raw edges, these will need to be folded to meet in the center of your strip and pressed with an iron to create a binding strip with finished edges. Premade bias binding may also be purchased from sewing supply shops if you don't wish to cut and fold your own binding.

2. There are many ways to bind an edge. This first example uses a straight-of-grain length of ¼-inch (6-mm) cotton tape, which will fold to produce an approximately ⅛-inch (3-mm) bound edge. The tape is placed on the edge so that approximately half of the tape overlaps the fabric, then this is tacked down with a felling stitch (page 63).

3. At the end, the fabric is flipped to the other side, the tape folded over the raw edge, and the second edge of the tape once again secured with a felling stitch. It is possible to attach binding by machine all in one go, stitching from the top side while simultaneously catching the underside, but this usually requires much practice; because you're not able to easily see the underside of the fabric, the edge often comes out unevenly stitched or the binding edge missed altogether.

(continued)

Right: Binding used to finish the seam allowance of a c. 1898—99 bodice

2a

2b

2c

3

Binding (Continued)

Alternative Method

This second method uses a strip of premade bias binding (also called double fold or bias tape), which has had both its edges folded in and pressed flat to hide the raw edges of the strip.

Steps

1. Unfold the strip and align it so that the edge of the binding aligns with the edge of the fabric. The inside of the binding should be facing upward. Stitch it to the fabric along the crease. This example is stitched with a small running stitch (page 55), but a backstitch (page 59), combination stitch (page 61), half backstitch (page 60) or machine stitch will work equally well.

2. At the end of the first seam, fold the binding over the raw edge and secure the underside in place. This example uses a felling stitch (page 63) to secure the second side, but this may also be done carefully with a machine stitch by stitching in the ditch between the binding and the fabric on the first side. The underside of the binding will be caught down while keeping the stitch on the outside discreet.

Turn and Fell

This is a method present in all manner of garments throughout many centuries of history, used to finish everything from hem edges to raw seam edges.

Two factors I have found most important to achieving a neat and narrow seam are the needle size and the working tension. Small, thin needles pass through fine fabric more easily and promote smaller stitches than do bulkier needles. I prefer to stitch with a #10 sharp for felling edges.

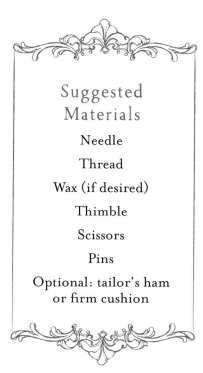

Suggested Materials

Needle

Thread

Wax (if desired)

Thimble

Scissors

Pins

Optional: tailor's ham or firm cushion

Left: The inside of a turned-and-felled hem on the neck edge of a hand-sewn c. 19th-century shift

Steps

1. To finish a hem edge by turning and felling, simply turn one edge of the fabric edge inward, then fold that edge inward once again so that the raw edge is fully concealed. The width of the fold will depend on your personal preference and ability. Narrower hems are much less conspicuous and therefore often more desirable, but these are more tedious to achieve.

2. The folded edge is held in place with whipstitches (also called felling stitches [page 63]). Begin with an anchoring stitch in the method of your choice (pages 83 and 84). The second stitch will determine the distance that you will need to repeat for the remainder of the seam to achieve even stitches, so try to be deliberate about deciding this.

3. Smaller stitches will be stronger but will result in more frequent dashes showing through to the right side of your material, whereas larger stitches will be slightly weaker but less noticeable from the right side of the garment, so the choice on stitch length is up to you, but I generally like to aim for between 6 and 12 stitches per inch (2.5 cm) depending on the task. It's best to try to take up as little of the ground fabric as possible to keep your front-facing stitches as small as possible, and to catch only the first couple of threads of the folded edge so that not too much of the slanted stitch is seen but that it sits fairly inconspicuously along the fold. If your garment has been interlined (flat lined), then it is best to try to catch only the interlining layer so that none of the felling stitches show through to the outside of the garment.

Turn and Fell (Continued)

Note:

Tensioning the seam is also crucial to achieving narrow felled seams, as the tension will help to keep the fold straight and neatly in place while you stitch it down. You'll find yourself starting to do this naturally with your hands, pulling the fabric between your fingers as you stitch. This can cause significant strain on your hands and will start to hurt after some time. When working a seam away from the body or horizontally, it's best to pin the work to a firm cushion or fold of heavy material so that you can use this to pull against and save your hands the strain. Having the work properly tensioned will also help you work a lot more quickly.

This method of working the stitch away from the body or horizontally is very common throughout earlier centuries; however, at some point during the 19th century, sewing instruction texts advise working toward the body, wrapping the seam around the index finger and tensioning with the thumb and middle finger. This method is also far less straining on the muscles of the hand and can be done for much longer periods of time without fatigue. Each method has its benefits and one may be more comfortable for you than the other; and while there is no strength difference between these methods, do note that the change in direction causes the slant of the felling stitches to fall in opposite directions, so those hoping to produce historical reconstructions may wish to take up the method more common in a particular period.

Whether you prefer vertical or horizontal stitching, stitching toward or away from you, I am personally not a proponent of the idea of "proper" or "improper" sewing technique. Just as people have the ability to work competently with left hands or right hands, so too I believe do we have the ability to stitch competently in any manner that we find comfortable. As long as you are able to stitch quickly and neatly in your preferred holding position and direction, then this is the correct method for you.

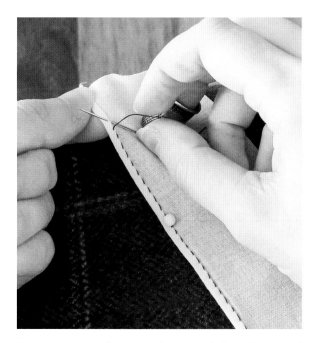

Pinning your work to a cushion can help add essential tension without hand fatigue.

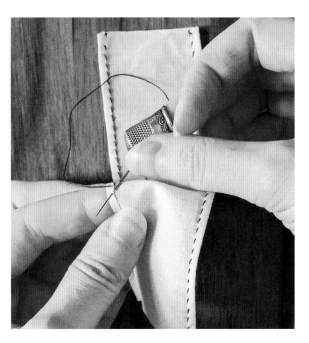

Nineteenth-century instruction favors wrapping the folded edge around a finger for tension and stitching with the needle pointed downward, toward the body.

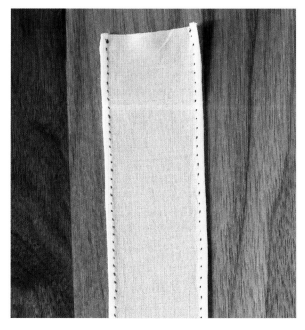

The opposite side of a felled edge: Smaller stitches make for more frequent marks (left edge) while larger stitches make for less frequent marks (right edge).

The underside of a backstitched seam is usually the direction in which a felled seam allowance will fold.

Turning and Felling Seam Allowances

Turning and felling seam allowance edges (otherwise known as flat felling) is much the same in terms of the stitching technique and the tensioning methods, but the edge must be prepared slightly differently before the stitch can be worked.

Suggested
Materials

Needle

Thread

Wax (if desired)

Thimble

Scissors

Pins

Optional: tailor's ham
or firm cushion

Steps

1. As there are two layers (and sometimes more) of material in a seam allowance instead of just the one in a hem, one layer of this must be trimmed away to lessen the bulk of the seam. The edge to be cut away will be the edge on the side in which the seam will lay; so, for example, if you wish to stitch your seam down to the right of the stitching line, you will need to trim the right side of the seam allowance. If you've backstitched (page 59) your seam, the direction of folding is usually toward the underside of the backstitch, so the longer and more prominent underside stitches are covered by the felled edge.

2. This should be trimmed to roughly half the width of the other side of the seam allowance so that this opposite edge may be folded around the raw edge and secured to the ground fabric with a felling stitch.

3. Once again, tension is crucial here, particularly as this will help you to keep the seam very flat. A loose or bubbled seam will create bulk, which can be avoided by both stitching the seam under tension as well as ensuring that you're keeping the underside of the seam (at the stitching line) pressed very flat with your fingers as you stitch.

A turned-and-felled seam allowance on a c. 19th-century hand-sewn shift, seen from the right side of the garment

Counter Hems

Counter hemming is fairly similar in technique to turning and felling, as the stitch worked for this is also a whipstitch. The difference is in the practical application, however. Whereas turning and felling is primarily used to finish edges, a counter hem is a method of seaming, used to connect two pieces of fabric to each other with finished edges. Rather than stitching two pieces of fabric with right sides together and then turning and felling the seam allowance, the technique of counter hemming requires each piece of fabric to be folded and felled to the other, once on the inside and once on the outside.

Suggested
Materials

Pins (optional)

Needle

Thread

Wax (if desired)

Thimble

Scissors

Steps

1. With both sides of your fabric placed with right sides facing up, a counter hem will require each piece to have a fold made in the opposite direction. So, for example, one piece of your fabric will be folded to the wrong side while the other is folded to the right side.

2. The pieces of fabric are then placed so that the folds interlock, while the right sides of the material are still both facing outward. I'd suggest placing pins along your seam as this first seam can be very fiddly to manage otherwise.

3. Beginning with an anchoring stitch (page 50), proceed to work a whipstitch (page 63) along the first edge, securing the one side of the fabric to the other.

4. When you reach the end of the first seam, either tie off your thread and restart on the underside, or if enough thread is remaining, pass the needle between the layers of material and bring it back up on the underside.

5. Continue working a whipstitch along this second edge, ensuring that you're keeping the seam taut and flat so that the finished seam isn't bubbled.

6. Your finished seam should look identical on both the inside and the outside, with one half showing the slanted whipstitches and the other showing the dashed stitches of the whipstitches on the opposite side.

As you might notice, counter hems are not inconspicuous seams. They place a noticeably thicker strip of fabric at the seam, and more stitches are visible from both the inside and the outside of the material. However, a counter hem is very durable and hard-wearing. They're often seen in extant garments at the shoulder seams of undershirts and workwear: places that often saw abrasive contact with heavier outer garments and that needed to withstand frequent washing.

Right: Counter hem visible on the shoulder seam of a c. 19th-century hand-sewn shift

French Seams

French seaming gained prevalence in historical dressmaking during the 19th century, likely due to the invention of the sewing machine and the speed that it allows. Because French seaming effectively requires each seam to be stitched twice, this is very time-consuming to do by hand.

French seams require at least ½ inch (1.3 cm) of seam allowance, if not more, as the first stitch will be made into the seam allowance width itself, so be sure to plan for this if you wish to French seam your garment.

Suggested Materials

Scissors

Pins

Sewing machine or needle

Thread

Wax (if desired)

Steps

1. French seams are worked in two stages. The first stage requires the fabric panels to be pinned together with the wrong sides facing.

2. Your first seam will be made slightly adjacent to the marked stitching line, about halfway onto the seam allowance width. The width of your seam allowance is up to you, but know that this distance will determine the width of the finished seam that will be left inside the garment. To make a narrow seam, stitch ⅛ to ¼ inch (3 to 6 mm) away from the stitching line; a wider seam can be stitched ½-inch (1.3-cm) distance or more.

3. The stitched seam is then pressed open. If the remaining seam allowance is greater than the distance between your stitching line and the marked line, or if your fabric has started to fray, this seam allowance will need to be trimmed back.

4. The panels are now folded back at the seam so that the right sides of the fabric pieces are now facing. This can be pressed again for a neater finish, and is once again pinned into place.

5. Stage two of this seam is to stitch now along the marked line, enclosing the raw seam allowance edge into the space between the first row of stitching and the second. Once again, it is essential that the raw width of seam allowance not exceed this distance, or that your fabric is not heavily fraying; otherwise, this will be caught in your seam and will show on the outside of your garment.

6. The seam is then pressed flat, with the inner seam allowance pressed to one side according to your preference.

A Matter of Pressing Importance

Pressing is arguably just as important as the sewing itself in the making of garments, and it's the secret to ensuring that your projects come out looking clean and professional. It's best to use an iron that can also steam, although it is possible to obtain neat seams without a built-in steam function. A spray bottle with water will be useful to gently dampen and relax any stubborn creases in nonsilk fabrics and is often a sufficient alternative to steam. It is also good to have a press cloth handy—a simple scrap of muslin or scrap cotton to lay between the garment and the iron will do—when pressing wools or fabrics that may become scorched by the iron. Do pay close attention to your heat settings: Whereas cottons and linens can withstand high temperatures, many synthetics will melt at the touch of the iron if the temperature is set too high, so do be sure to test your heat settings on a piece of cabbage (scrap fabric) before pressing your actual seams.

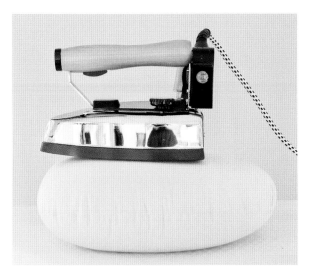

Pressing tools

As a general rule, it's best to press every seam as soon as it's sewn. In most cases, this is simply a matter of pressing the seam allowances open to achieve the flattest press of the seam, but some seams—such as French seams—will require the seam to be pressed to one side or the other.

While it is possible to carefully press the more tricky portions of a garment, such as sleeves and curved seams on a flat surface, these tasks may be assisted by specialty pressing tools that are purpose-built to solve unique pressing tasks.

A tailor's ham is used to press curved darts

A tailor's ham is probably the most versatile and will see the most frequent use. This allows you to mold a curved seam or dart around the variously sized curves of the ham to achieve cleanly pressed curved seams.

A sleeve board

Sleeve boards can assist in the pressing of sleeves, as these provide a slim surface to slide into the sleeve so that it can be pressed in the round without the vertical creases inevitable when pressing sleeves flat.

A tailor's clapper—which is essentially a heavy wooden block—will help you obtain very flat and neat seams since the wood will help to absorb the heat of the iron, setting the fold of the fabric faster. This block should be applied with pressure to a seam immediately after the iron is removed as the fabric cools. A clapper may also act as a substitute for a hot iron on more delicate pressing tasks: After steaming, the clapper may be applied to flatten a seam without risking heat damage that may be incurred with an iron.

Pressing Velvet

Fabrics that have standing piles, such as velvets and velveteens, cannot be ironed flat without crushing the pile and thus altering the natural texture of the fabric. To press seams on fabrics with standing piles, these piles will need to be supported by placing the fabric face down on either another piece of velvet or velveteen, or on a purpose-made velvet board that is covered in needles to support the plush. The fabric will then be pressed from the wrong side, which will usually be plain-woven without a pile. This method allows you to press neat seams into your garment while still preserving the standing pile on the right side of the fabric.

Closures

It's remarkable how, despite today's innovations of high-stretch materials, zippers, snaps and Velcro, the methods used to close garments throughout centuries of history still remain in ready use today: We lace our shoes just as we laced corsets; our dresses, skirts and trousers still close with hooks and eyes; we button our coats the way that we buttoned coats, sleeves, doublets and gowns for centuries. Closures are essential to making sure that our clothes stay fastened, and as points that are often made to take significant strain, very often require a bit of maintenance.

In this section, we'll be exploring some of the methods by which clothes were fastened up through the turn of the 20th century, all of which are very easily done by hand. With the exception of the buttonhole setting on many modern domestic sewing machines, most of these techniques are impossible to do with domestic machinery, so get your thimble ready.

Buttonhole Stitch

First and foremost, it's important to understand the buttonhole stitch, as this is used in instances beyond just the buttonhole and will feature in several of the closure methods to follow. This effectively involves tying a series of small knots with each stitch.

Suggested
Materials

Needle

Thread (preferably
buttonhole twist)

Wax (if desired)

Thimble

Scissors

Steps

1. To work a buttonhole stitch, first insert your needle at your starting point.

2. Next, wrap the tail thread attached to the needle end so that the thread passes under the needle from left to right. This effectively forms a loop through which the thread will pass to form a knot.

3. Pull the needle and thread tight to form the knot. Note: The thread should be pulled in the direction in which you wish the knot to sit, and the thread should always be pulled in the same direction in a series of stitches so that the knots sit evenly. Usually the knot will need to sit at the edge of the material to add strength or protection, so for a buttonhole, the thread should always be pulled toward the edge of the cut.

Left: Buttonholes worked on a c. 1880s silk bodice. The buttons have been cut away and repurposed.

Buttonholes

Buttonholes are best worked through two or more layers of material and with a heavy thread, since these will usually see lots of wear and strain. Silk thread is the strongest and therefore preferable; there is a reason that "silk twist" thread is often called "buttonhole twist" due to its historically common usage in working buttonholes. Buttonholes may be done using a single or double thread, depending on the weight of the fabric used; doubled thread will make for much quicker stitching, but single threads may appear more delicate and may be preferable for lighter garments.

There are two types of buttonhole: a straight buttonhole and a keyhole buttonhole. This latter style involves adding a small circular opening to one end of the buttonhole marking to allow a button to sit in the hole more comfortably. This is often done on heavier garments such as coats and jackets, but is not common on lighter garments such as shirts. A small hole is punched, cut or pushed with an awl into the side of the buttonhole that the button will pull against; on coats, this is usually toward the outer edge.

The direction in which you work is up to you and depends on your dominant hand. This right-handed demonstration works from left to right and with the needle pointing downward, according to 1895 demonstrations[11] but this can just as easily be done working from the top edge.

(continued)

Suggested Materials

Ruler

Fabric marking tool (pencil, chalk or disappearing ink)

Scissors or buttonhole chisel

Needle

Thread (preferably buttonhole twist)

Wax (if desired)

Thimble

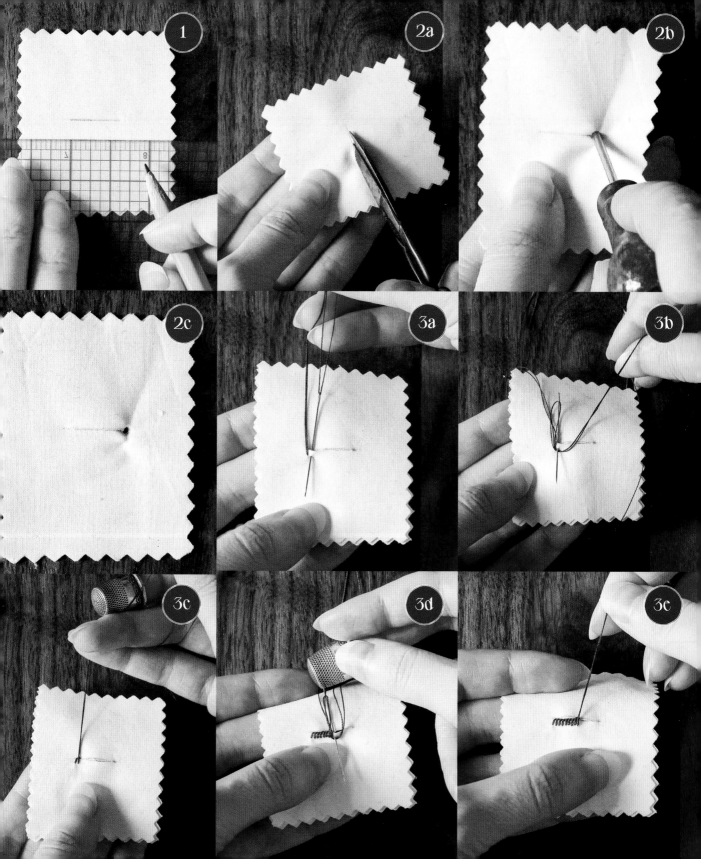

Buttonholes (Continued)

Steps

1. To begin a standard buttonhole, first mark out the width you'll need the opening to be. This should sit as straight across the weave of the fabric as possible, although this may not always be clear on more complex weaves, such as brocades or twills.

2. The horizontal marking is then gently cut either with a pair of small scissors or with a designated buttonhole chisel. Once again, try to ensure that you're making as straight a cut as possible since your buttonhole will not appear as neat if too many of the horizontal threads are cut. If your fabric is particularly wobbly, it may be helpful to put a small basting stitch around your marked line to stabilize the material. If you're working a keyhole buttonhole, work a small hole at one end of the marked line with an awl.

3. Work evenly spaced buttonhole stitches (page 99) along this first raw edge to seal and protect it from wear. The depth taken for each stitch is up to you and depends both on the thickness of the material and the aesthetic preference of the buttonhole. Just be sure to stick to whatever depth you do decide on, to ensure that your binding threads appear even in length.

4. When you reach the end of your first long edge, you'll want to add a worked bar across the short end to keep your buttonhole from stretching out. To do this, insert the needle into the unworked side of your buttonhole at the depth you'll be making the rest of the stitches. Bring the needle back up next to the bottom of your last stitch on the worked side of the buttonhole. This will create a long thread running from one end of the buttonhole to the other.

5. Proceed to buttonhole stitch along this horizontal thread, catching a bit of the ground fabric as well, so that the worked bar is anchored to the fabric and doesn't float free. Place approximately two stitches on one side of the cut, one stitch precisely in the middle, and two stitches again on the other side of the cut. This may be adapted depending on the depth of your stitches—some buttonholes may require seven stitches (three on each side and one in the middle) or three.

6. If you're working a keyhole buttonhole, this first turning point will be rounded, so a worked bar will not be needed. Simply continue buttonhole stitching along the rounded edge until the opposite edge of the buttonhole edge is reached.

7. Proceed along the second edge in the same way as you did the first.

8. When you reach the second short edge, place another worked bar along this edge.

9. Once you've finished your second bar, pass your needle to the underside of the work and finish off your thread.

Tip:

Everyone, no matter how experienced with buttonholes, usually requires a couple of warm-up buttonholes before having a go at the real thing. Each buttonhole job requires unique spacing and stitch length according to fabric and thread weights, so starting with a few warm-up buttonholes is always in your best interest, no matter what your sewing skill level might be. You may find that your first few buttonholes go a bit slowly, but they do become much quicker as you work into a rhythm and start to adapt your muscle memory to your specific stitch length and spacing. It's best to try to do as many of your buttonholes in a single sitting as you can manage, since you'll be able to work up a speed and neatness with repetition.

Button Loops

This method of closing a garment with buttons is similar to the buttonhole method in terms of the stitching technique, only these buttonhole stitches are worked on an external thread loop instead of into the fabric itself. This method may be preferable in circumstances where the closure point is uncertain or may need to be changed in the future; a thread loop can be clipped and remade elsewhere, but a buttonhole cut into the fabric cannot be closed inconspicuously later.

Suggested Materials

Needle

Thread (usually heavy weight or buttonhole twist)

Wax (if desired)

Thimble

Scissors

Steps

1. After anchoring your thread (page 50) on the wrong side of your garment, bring the needle up to the right side, then back down to the wrong side. Do not pull the thread flat, but leave enough of a loop so that your button can pass through easily without slipping free. Ensure that the loop is very snug around the button as it will stretch slightly as you work the buttonhole stitches around. It is recommended to use doubled thick thread (preferably buttonhole twist) for strength. Once you have determined the size of your loop, secure your thread on the wrong side of the garment with a backstitch (page 59) or knot to prevent the loop from adjusting size.

2. Bring the needle back up to the right side of the garment at the base of your thread loop.

3. Beginning at the base of the loop, slip your needle halfway under the thread loop, then work a buttonhole stitch (page 99).

4. Proceed to buttonhole stitch along the thread loop, ensuring that the knots are packed tightly together and that you're pulling the knots in the same direction with each stitch so that they sit flush with one another.

5. Continue in this manner along the entire thread loop to reinforce it with an even row of buttonhole stitches.

Making Buttons from Your Fabric

There are practically infinite ways to construct buttons, including many intricate thread wrapping techniques requiring an entire text of their own, but we'll start with the essentials here. This technique of constructing round buttons has been around since at least the medieval period, and remains an excellent method for making up buttons in the fabric of your choice, whether you wish to match the garment you're intending to button, or to instead contrast with something special.

These buttons can be made up in any size, but I find the British one-pound coin or U.S. quarter to be my go-to button size. Feel free to experiment with the currency size of your choice.

Steps

1. Trace around your small round object with pencil or chalk.

2. Cut a little ways outside of your marked line to provide a bit of seam allowance. This should be fairly narrow unless the fabric you're working with is very prone to fraying.

3. Next, work a gathering thread (an unanchored running stitch [page 56]) along your marked line. These stitches should be fairly small so that the button will gather up more neatly.

4. For this next step, you'll need a bit of stuffing to pad the buttons out. Personally, I prefer to take this opportunity to put some cabbage (scrap fabric) and thread clippings to use; these are chopped up very finely, as you don't want the chunks to be too big and pointy or they may distort the shape of your button, especially if you're using a fine outer fabric.

Suggested Materials

Marking tool (pencil, chalk or disappearing ink)

Small round object for tracing (such as a £1 or 25¢ coin)

Scissors

Fabric for buttons

Needle

Thread

Wax (if desired)

Thimble

Stuffing for buttons (cotton, wool, poly-fil, thread clippings or scrap fabric)

5. Place a small (approximately pea-sized) amount of stuffing in the middle of your button circle.

6. Pull the gathering thread so that the circle is drawn up to enclose the stuffing. You may at this point wish to clip away some of your seam allowance so that only about ⅛ inch (3 mm) remains.

7. Do your best to tuck the raw edges of your seam allowance into the button, and stitch across this opening to seal it up. This step works best on wool fabrics, as wool can felt and seal up nicely.

Attaching Buttons

Now, to stitch your freshly made button to your garment.

Suggested
Materials

Needle

Thread (preferably
buttonhole twist)

Wax (if desired)

Thimble

Scissors

Fabric button(s)

Steps

1. Holding your button in the correct position from the right side of the material, anchor your thread (page 50) on the wrong side and pass the needle a few times across this underside, catching the material of the button from the right side.

2. Once the button is secure, pass the needle up to the right side of the fabric.

3. Wrap the thread several times tightly around the base of the button or work a buttonhole stitch (page 99) around the base of the button to raise it slightly from the material and to give the buttonhole side of the fabric some room to sit comfortably underneath.

4. Pass the needle back to the underside of the garment to finish your stitch.

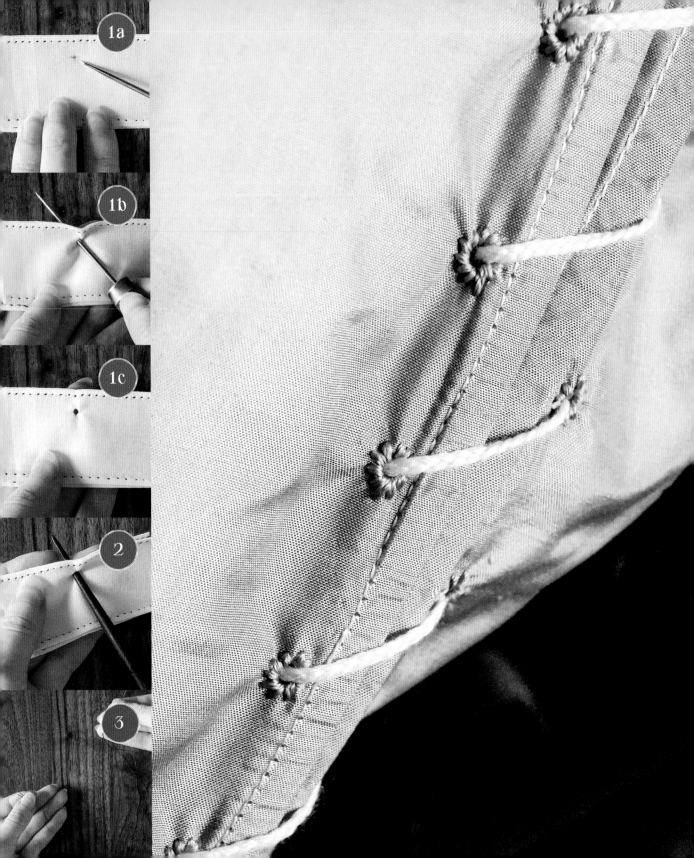

Eyelets

The purpose of eyelets is to hold open a hole in a piece of fabric so that a lacing cord or ribbon may pass through to close or attach two pieces of a garment. Metal grommets were only introduced into garment construction in the early 19th century, so eyelet holes in the centuries before needed to be worked by hand. This is a relatively straightforward and often relaxing task that can become very fast and efficient with some practice.

Suggested Materials

Marking tool (pencil, chalk, disappearing ink)

Awl, or tapered tool such as a sharp pencil or hair stick

Needle

Thread (preferably buttonhole twist)

Wax (if desired)

Thimble

Scissors

Steps

1. As with buttonholes, it is best to work eyelet holes through at least two layers of material so that they're well stabilized, especially as these are going to take strain when laced. To work an eyelet hole, begin first by marking out where you'd like your eyelet holes to be, as these are difficult if not sometimes impossible to revert once put in. At each marking point, first gently separate the weave of the material with an awl or other pointed object.

2. Once a hole has been established, it may then be necessary to go through and widen this hole with a tapered awl (or a pencil will often work just as well) if your eyelet hole needs to be a bit larger. Do your best only to stretch the weave of the material rather than break the threads, as this will weaken the eyelet hole, especially if you're working yours by hand rather than adding a metal grommet. Some threads may break naturally in the widening process, especially if you're using a fabric woven from weaker yarns; this is usually okay and won't ruin your project. It's best to avoid *cutting* holes into your fabric, though, unless you're setting wide metal grommets.

3. It's best to use a thick and strong thread for eyelets, as these will see significant wear with the passing of lacing cords and potential tightening. Heavy silk twist was a common choice historically, but any thick thread will work for today. (Thinner threads can be used, but will take longer to work since you'll be able to cover less surface area with a single stitch. Thin threads may be necessary for lighter materials, however, if subtlety is required of an eyelet.)

(continued)

Eyelets (Continued)

4. I prefer to thread my needle double for this purpose to help the process move a bit quicker. Beginning from the wrong side of the garment, bury the ends of the thread between the two layers of material, then anchor it near the edge of the hole either with a backstitch (page 59), knot or buttonhole stitch (page 99).

5. The garment is then flipped to the right side, and the needle passed up through the hole.

6. The needle is inserted a little ways below the hole and brought up once again through the hole opening so that the thread pulls back and binds off the edge of the hole. Pay close attention to the distance you're placing the needle from the edge of the hole since you'll need to replicate this as precisely as possible while passing around the rest of the hole to ensure a neat eyelet. Do also be aware that the thread will draw the edge of the hole a bit wider as you pull it taut, so the distance you place your needle away from the hole will shrink slightly.

7. This process is repeated incrementally around the remainder of the hole. Ensure that no edges of the hole remain exposed, but you don't need to spend too much time filling in all the spaces along the outer edge of the eyelet. Some spacing between the outer edge stitches is natural and is present in historical garments, forming a small starburst rather than a solid dough-nut. Fewer stitches taken means less time needed to complete an eyelet.

8. Once you reach the starting point, pass the needle back to the underside of the garment, and anchor off the thread.

9. You may then need to go in and stretch this hole again if you find that the fabric has closed up a bit during stitching.

Speed tip:

If you're doing a series of eyelets, you can save a bit of time by not knotting off the thread after finishing each eyelet, but instead passing the thread down to the next point and continuing your eyeleting endeavors from there. This is a hack that can be found on extant garments at least as far back as the 18th century. Just be sure that you have enough thread left to complete the full next eyelet before proceeding.

Lacing Patterns

Two of the most prevalent lacing patterns throughout history are cross lacing and spiral lacing. Cross lacing is the style we're most familiar with in our modern day, whereby two ends of a lacing cord are worked simultaneously and are made to cross over each other to form a column of orderly Xs. Cross lacing was exceedingly rare in historical garments before the 19th century, however, with most laced garments being closed by the spiral lacing method instead. Spiral lacing involves passing a single end of a lacing cord through a series of offset holes in an ascending or descending spiral pattern. As there is no lacing cord passing between the opening edges of the garment, spiral lacing allows a garment to shut completely, with both edges of the garment sitting flush against one another.

The eyelet hole layout must be worked slightly differently for spiral lacing than for cross lacing, so do be sure to plan for this if you hope to spiral lace your garment instead of cross lacing it. If your lacing holes are very close together, then the offsetting doesn't matter so much structurally and you can get away with parallel lacing holes in most cases; but if your lacing holes are to be more spaced out, they must be worked in an offset pattern to avoid pulling the garment diagonally. For the lacing to start and finish neatly, there must be additional holes worked a half distance away from the starting bottom hole and the finishing top hole (which will be on opposite sides of the garment).

Cross lacing   Spiral lacing

Suggested Materials

Lacing, ribbon or cord

A bodkin or large tapestry needle if working with fine cords and small lacing holes

Spiral Lacing Steps

1. To lace a garment in the spiral lacing method, begin by inserting your lacing cord from inside to outside, and tying a large knot to stop the cord from pulling through.

2. Proceed to the lacing hole on the opposite side of the garment, inserting the cord from outside to inside.

3. Proceed back to the first side of the garment and insert the lacing cord once again from inside to outside.

4. Repeat this process, ensuring that the lacing cord does not cross through the edge of the garment so as not to obstruct the ability of the edges to sit flush. When lacing through narrow eyelet holes with fine cord, you may wish to use a thick tapestry needle or bodkin to assist with getting the cord through the holes.

(continued)

Lacing Patterns (Continued)

5. At the top of the garment, pass the lacing cord through the final hole, which should be positioned a half distance away from the previous hole on the same side; this final set of holes should be on the opposite side from the pair on the starting side so that the lacing will finish on the inside of the garment.

6. Tie a knot at the base of the hole to prevent the lacing cord from slipping through, and tuck any remaining cord between the garment and the body.

Cross Lacing Steps

This is one of several methods of cross lacing, but the one most commonly used in corsetry.

1. Beginning with a long lacing cord (4 yards or meters will usually suffice unless a large lacing gap is desired), locate the halfway point.

2. Thread either end of the lacing cord through the first set of eyelets, pulling so that the halfway point on your cord sits exactly centered. This step may be done either by inserting the cords from the front of the garment to exit through the back, or from the back of the garment to exit from the front. It doesn't matter which you do, but it is generally best to begin in the manner that will leave your final pair of lacing holes threading from outside to inside so that the knot sits to the inside.

3. Crossing each end of the lace over to the opposite side, thread through the next pair of holes. If your lacing cord has exited through the back of the garment in the previous set, you will need to enter through the back on the next set of holes; a front-exiting lace will need to enter through the front on the next set of holes.

4. Repeat this process down each set of holes, crossing the laces and ensuring that they enter each new set of holes according to the side exited in the previous step.

5. For corsets: When you reach the sets of holes directly at waist level, it is useful to add tightening loops so that the tightest pull is at the waist (not, more uncomfortably, at the hips or up near the lungs), and so that you can adjust the corset without having to untie the whole thing. This is done by exiting the cord at the first set of waist-level holes, then directly entering the next set of holes on the same side *without crossing over*. Do not pull this tightly, but allow long loops to form. You'll be able to pull these to tighten and loosen the lacing as you please. Leave just enough extra cord to finish the rest of your lacing.

6. When you reach the bottom, knot both ends of your cord together. Pull any extra slack back into the lacing and up toward the tightening loops.

Hooks & Eyes

Hook-and-eye or hook-and-bar closures saw a great rise in popularity throughout the 19th century, and they are still widely used in garment construction today. Whether you're looking to add a discreet closure to a new sewing project or you need to repair a loose hook on an existing garment, this is a very handy closure technique that doesn't take too much time. As with most closures, it's best to work hooks and eyes on portions of a garment that have been layered with two or more layers of fabric, as these will pull and cause strain.

First, it will be important to distinguish whether you'll need to use an eye (rounded) or a bar (straight). An eye should be used to close two edges that must sit flush against each other. The eye will facilitate this, as it can be stitched well onto the fabric while only a small space protrudes over the edge for the hook to catch. A bar, on the other hand, should be used where a finished hook edge must overlap another piece of fabric. Because the stitching points on a bar are on the same plane as the point where the hook will catch, the closure will not be seen when the garment is fastened.

Packages of hooks and eyes generally also come with bars provided, but bars and eyes may also be worked by hand with thread in the absence of metal options. Worked bars are useful not only as hook closure points, but can also be added to garments as belt loops or to reinforce vulnerable junctions, such as shirt slits or at the skirts of some 17th- and 18th-century stays.[12]

(continued)

Left: Back closure of an evening bodice, c. 1860. These hooks have been very hastily sewn on, proving that perfection has never been required to produce perfectly functional garments.

Suggested Materials

Needle (short needles work best for this)

Thread (use buttonhole twist for extra strength)

Wax (if desired)

Thimble

Marking tool (pencil, chalk or disappearing ink)

Scissors

Hooks

Eyes or bars (optional—if you don't wish to work your own thread bar)

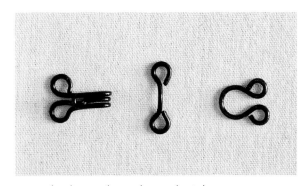

Hook (left), bar (center), eye (right)

Hooks & Eyes (Continued)

Worked Bar Closure Steps

1. To add a worked bar to your garment, first anchor (page 103) your doubled thread (page 50) on the wrong side of the material and bring the needle up to the right side at the point where you'd like your bar to start.

2. Bring your needle back down at the length you'd like your bar to be. A worked bar for a hook is generally about ¼ inch (6 mm) long, but belt loops may need to be longer to accommodate the width of the belt. Worked bars for hooks should be pulled fairly tightly but should not warp the fabric; belt loops may need to have a bit of ease, but keep in mind that these loops do tend to stretch a bit as the bar is worked.

3. Take a backstitch on the wrong side of the material where the needle has been pulled through to secure the length, then bring the needle back up to the right side at the entry point of the thread.

4. Proceed to work rows of buttonhole stitches along the length of your ground thread. (See the section on buttonhole stitching [page 99] for a detailed walkthrough of this.)

5. When you reach the end of your bar, finish off your thread on the wrong side of the garment.

(continued)

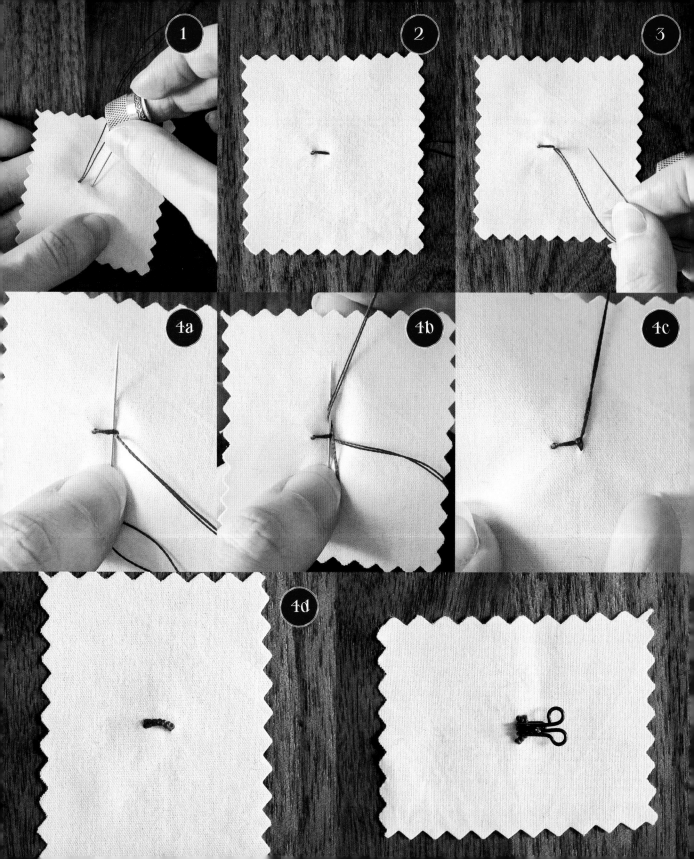

Hooks & Eyes (Continued)

Hook Closure Steps

1. To add a hook to a garment, first place the hook in position according to your desired closure point. If a hook is intended to meet an eye for an edge-to-edge closure, the curve of the hook should sit perfectly flush with the edge of the material. If the hook is too far in, the edge of the fabric will have to fold to be able to close; if it is placed too far out, the end of the hook will be seen when the garment is fastened.

2. The simplest way to attach a hook is to place a series of whipstitches (page 63) along the rounded fastening points. Ideally, these should be wrapped neatly, but extant hook-and-eye sewing is often done very hastily to conserve time; these hooks are rarely seen, so neatness isn't technically a priority if you don't fancy it.

3. When you reach the end of the second loop, pass your needle under the first layer of fabric to come up again just near the crook.

4. Pass the thread across the hook and bring the needle back down to finish it off. This stitch will help to hold the hook flat and prevent it from flipping forward.

5. When placing an eye on a garment that is meant to meet edge to edge, the eye should extend approximately 1 mm past the edge of the fabric—just enough so that the hook will be able to pass through but not enough so that the eye will show too much when the garment is fastened.

6. If you're feeling fancy or want your hooks and eyes to be especially secure, alternatively these may be secured with a series of buttonhole stitches instead of whipstitches (see buttonhole stitching [page 99] for a detailed explanation of this stitch).

A Little Something Special

While not strictly essential to the structural integrity of clothing, the following techniques not only provide a bit of additional visual interest, but they also have their varying practical uses as well: Gathering, pleating and smocking provide a method of fitting longer widths of fabric into smaller spaces, providing shape to a garment or, in the case of smocking, a bit of stretch; insertion techniques can give you the ability to add width or length to an existing garment or pattern.

Pleats

Pleating is a method of consolidating a longer length of fabric into a smaller band or other portion of a garment in a manner that is slightly flatter than gathering. Here, we'll be exploring the two fundamental methods of pleating: knife pleating, which is a directional form of pleating, and box pleating, which creates nondirectional, symmetrical folds.

Suggested Materials

Marking tool (pencil, chalk or disappearing ink)

Ruler

Pins

Needle

Thread

Wax (if desired)

Thimble

Iron

(continued)

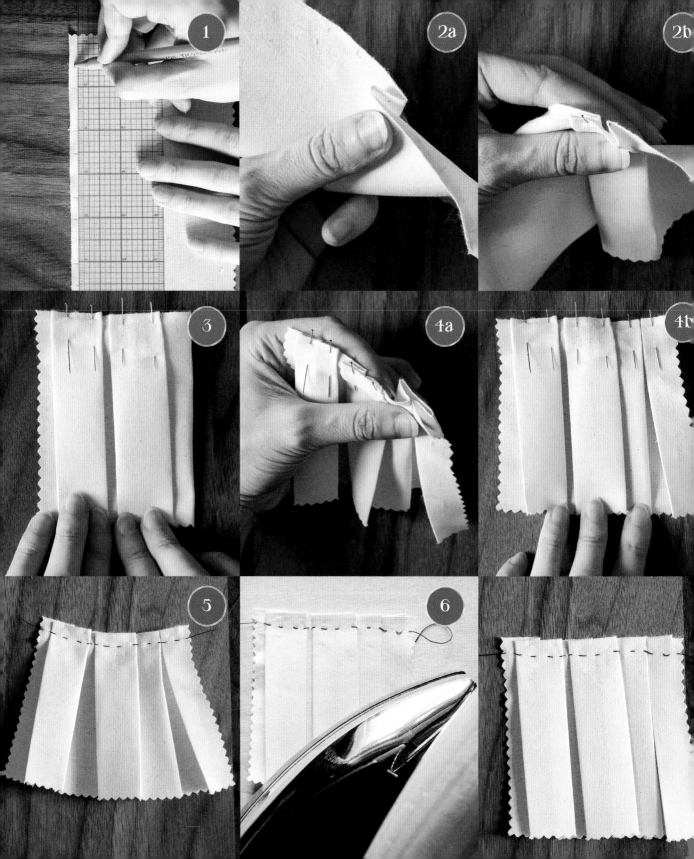

Pleats (Continued)

Knife Pleats Steps
(See photos on page 125)

1. To add knife pleats into your fabric, you'll first need to mark out where you want the fabric to be folded. Each pleat section should measure double the width that you wish the actual pleat to be. In this example, I'm marking 1-inch (2.5-cm) spaces that will be folded to form ½-inch (1.3-cm) pleats. Note that every other marking space will be a pleat; the alternate spaces will be the spacing distances between pleats, which can either be the same width as your pleat marking (so that there will be a small space between pleats), or this can be made wider or smaller as you prefer. Do keep in mind that part of your spacing will be covered by the previous pleat, so be sure to account for this. For example, if you want a ½-inch (1.3-cm) space before the fold of the next pleat, be sure to add your pleat width to this. If your pleats are ½ inch (1.3 cm), your spacing will need to measure 1 inch (2.5 cm) to leave ½ inch (1.3 cm) of spacing.

2. To fold the pleats, match up two of the markings, fold down the pleat to either side as you prefer, and pin.

3. The top edge of the pleated panel is then basted to hold the pleats in place.

4. The pleats are then usually ironed to crease them flat, although some may wish to skip this step for the aesthetic preference.

Box Pleats Steps

1. The pattern for marking box pleats onto your fabric is as follows: The width of the pleat will first be marked out at its finished width; in this example, I have marked out a 1-inch (2.5-cm) box pleat. On either side of the primary pleat will be marked the width of the fold, which will measure half the width of the primary pleat; in this example, this measures ½ inch (12 mm). On either side of these fold sections will be spacing distances. These may measure the same width as the primary pleat if you wish your box pleats to meet edge to edge with no spacing, but additional width can be added if some spacing is desired. Repeat this pattern until the desired number of pleats is reached.

2. To form the box pleats, fold each of the half-width under-pleats back behind the primary pleat so that they meet in the back.

3. These can be pinned to hold them temporarily in place.

4. Alternatively, an inverted box pleat can be worked, if preferred. This is achieved by folding the two half-width sections on top of the primary pleat so that they meet at the center of the full width.

5. The pleated section is basted across the top to hold the pleats in place.

6. The pleats are then usually ironed to press them flat.

Gathers

Gathers are an excellent way to consolidate a length of fabric into a shorter space; for example, when a full skirt is needed to fit into a smaller waistband or a large sleeve is needed to fit into a smaller cuff or armhole. Standard gathers may be worked in several ways, either with hand methods, such as whip or running stitches, or by machine with a straight stitch and without backstitching at the start or stop. When gathering, it's best to use as strong of a thread as possible so that it doesn't break when you're drawing up the fabric. I'm using silk buttonhole twist for these examples, as silk thread is one of the stronger options, and the buttonhole twist is thicker than standard silk threads, although a thinner thread may be desired for lighter fabrics as these will be easier to gather and put less strain on the fabric.

When gathering long lengths, such as hem ruffles, it may be wise to run your gathering threads in segments rather than stitching a whole length all the way around (if stitching by machine, that is; this would be rather impossible to do with hand stitching). As a general rule, it is best not to make a gathering thread travel more than one yard (1 m) in length. This way, if your thread breaks at any point, you don't have to regather the entire length of fabric but only the single segment that has broken.

Whipped Gathers Steps

Whipped gathers are seen most commonly in dressmaking before the 19th century and are fairly quick and simple to achieve.

1. Begin by inserting your needle at the desired starting point *without* anchoring your thread. The stitch should not be placed too deep into the seam as to be intrusive of your stitching line, but should be deep enough that the whipstitches will not pull the threads out of the weave if you're working along a raw edge.

2. Proceed to work a whipstitch (page 63) along the edge that you wish to gather. The size of your stitches will depend on how finely you'd like the finished gathers to be: Smaller stitches will mean finer gathers, which will only work on thin fabrics; wider stitches should be made for thicker gathers, which will be more suitable for heavier fabrics.

3. Once the gathering thread has been completed, one end of the thread can be gently pulled to gather up the material. Keep an eye on the other end of the thread, though; you don't want to accidentally push the material off the other end and lose your gathering thread.

(continued)

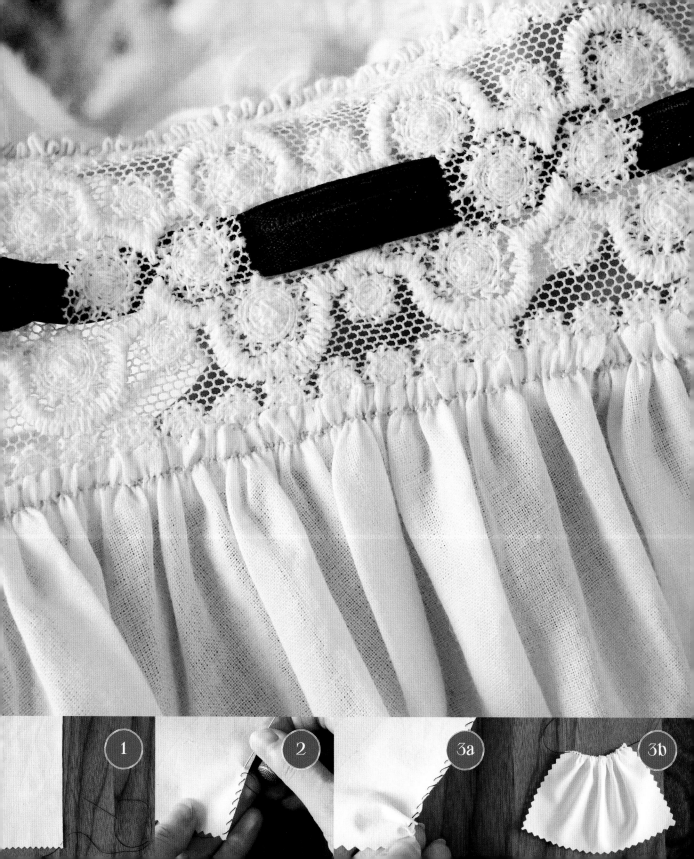

Gathers (Continued)

Running Gathers Steps

Running gathers gained popularity in the 19th century and are the method most commonly used today. This can be achieved either by working the running stitches by hand, or can be achieved more quickly by machine with a straight stitch on the longest stitch length setting.

1. If working by hand, begin your thread without anchoring your thread. Likewise if working by machine, a gathering thread should not be started or finished with a backstitch.

2. Proceed to work a running stitch (page 55) along the edge to be gathered. The amount of thread picked up by the needle should be approximately half the space of the fabric passed over per stitch. Using thread count as an example (although there are no rules as to how many threads per stitch makes a proper gathering stitch), the needle will take up two threads for every four passed over.

3. The size of your stitch will depend on how thick you'd like the gather folds to be: Larger stitches will produce bigger folds while smaller stitches will produce smaller folds. Small stitches will look beautiful on finer fabrics, but will be wasted on thicker fabrics as the material will only be able to fold so finely. Do be sure that, whichever size you choose, your stitches are regular enough to ensure that the gathers will come out uniformly.

4. A gathering thread will be sufficient with only a single row of running stitches, but a double row will ensure that the gathers lay a bit neater. The second row should be worked to match the first row exactly, with the thread entering and exiting at the exact points as the thread in the first row so that the fabric will gather up into neat folds.

5. The thread ends can then be pulled to draw up the fabric into gathers. Do be sure to keep an eye on the other end of the thread though so that you don't accidentally push your material off the other end.

6. When attaching a gathered piece of material to another piece of fabric, the gathers will first need to be stroked to ensure that they sit evenly. This is best done with a pin, gently sorting each fold so that they sit parallel and uniformly in size. The valley of each fold (or every couple of folds when working with a longer length of material) may be pinned to the ground fabric. This example illustrates the attachment of a cuff or finished waistband: With the right sides of both gathered material and cuff piece facing one another, the edges are lined up and the gathering piece pinned to the straight cuff.

7. I prefer to attach gathered pieces with backstitches (page 59) so that I can ensure that every length of every fold is secured with thread (with running stitches there will be gaps in your thread coverage that may leave some of the gathered folds vulnerable to undoing). The needle is inserted in the valley of one fold, then brought up in the valley of the next, then reinserted where the thread exited from the valley of the previous fold, and so on, pinning down each of your folds to the ground fabric.

(continued)

Gathers (Continued)

8. For the purposes of this cuff example, the edge is finished by folding the raw edge of the cuff piece in, and then folding that piece in half again to lay against the gathered edge and to conceal that raw edge.

9. This can then be secured with a felling stitch, with each stitch catching each bump in the gathered fabric.

Front   *Back*

Cartridge Pleating Steps

Cartridge pleating is a bit deceptively named, as the method for working this stitch is closer to that of gathering than pleating. Cartridge pleating is done much the same as in the running gathers method, although generally, cartridge pleats are meant to work much longer or heavier lengths of fabric into smaller spaces and so the stitches are to be worked a bit bigger.

1. Begin by working a long running stitch (page 55) near the edge of your material without first anchoring the thread. The size of your stitches is up to you, but keep in mind that longer stitches will produce thicker folds, whereas smaller stitches will produce shallower folds. Unlike in running gathers, these stitches should be even, with equal amounts of space taken up as passed over.

2. Cartridge pleating is worked with at least three rows of parallel gathering threads since these folds tend to be a bit bigger and therefore heavier, and will require a bit of extra support to keep them in shape. Each row of gathering should be worked exactly the same as the one above, so the needle enters and exits the fabric at the same points to ensure that the fabric can be drawn up into straight folds.

3. The ends of the threads are then pulled to draw up the fabric. These may need to be knotted when the desired folding configuration is achieved as the fabric may want to slide undone until it can be stitched onto a band or into a garment.

4. When attaching cartridge pleating to a band or other piece of fabric, the edges of the material are aligned before each fold is connected with a whipstitch (page 63) to the base material. The outer end of the fold is left free.

Lace Insertion

I've called this "lace" insertion since this is what was typically used as the material of insertion by the late 19th century, but this technique can just as easily be achieved with contrast fabrics, embroidered panels or other decorative materials to creatively add length or width to a garment.

The Decorative Method

This method was commonly used up through the early 20th century to add decorative lace strips and cutout details to garments. Because it involves overlaying the insertion material over an existing panel of fabric and then cutting away underneath, this method won't alter the size or length of your garment.

Decorative Method Steps
(See photos on page 136)

1. Begin by determining where on your fabric you'd like the lace to sit by positioning it on the outside of your garment or fabric panel. Make sure it's lying straight and symmetrically, if that's what you're going for.

2. The insertion will need to be temporarily secured in place so that it doesn't move out of position before you get to stitch it down. This can be done quickly with pins, but it's going to be more secure (and more accurate, as the pins warp the fabric slightly) if the strip is then basted into place with a pad stitch (page 69).

Suggested
Materials

Pins

Needle

Thread

Wax (if desired)

Thimble

Scissors

3. Proceed to stitch down either side of the lace by hand or by machine as you prefer. The combination stitch (running backstitch [page 61]) is used in this example for the speed of the running stitch with the additional bit of strength provided by the backstitch. Note that a contrasting thread is used in this example for visibility, but the thread should either match your garment, or a more regular stitch such as a running (page 55), back (page 59) or half backstitch (page 60) should be used instead if the thread is intended to be seen.

(continued)

The Decorative Method (Continued)

4. Flip over your garment to the wrong side and make a cut down the middle of the ground fabric. Be extra careful that you're only catching the ground fabric and you aren't cutting through the insertion layer.

5. The seam allowances may need to be trimmed if you're using a very wide insertion; they should not be excessively long or they may not want to sit back naturally; I would personally advise that seam allowances on insertion lace not exceed more than ½ inch (1.3 cm) in width. Historically, these edges were often left unfinished and raw; this may be done if the fabric used is very tightly woven, such as fine cotton, a wool that will felt or fabrics that are not prone to fraying such as many knits or felts. Otherwise, the edges may be finished as you prefer, whether by overlocking (serging), overcasting (page 79), pinking (page 76) or turning and felling (page 85).

6. The seam allowance edges will then need to be tacked back so that they don't flop forward and interfere with the decorative space left by the lace. This can be done as you prefer, either by running a machine stitch immediately next to the lace edge or working this stitch by hand. This example uses a running stitch (page 55) purely for speed as this secondary row of stitching is not structural.

The Resizing Method

This method requires either two separate garment panels that have not yet been sewn, or for the pieces of an existing garment to be unpicked along the seam where the insertion is to be placed. As this will be taking the place of the original seam, the new width of the decorative material will add that respective amount of room to the garment. This can be used to advantage when this resizing is desired, but do be sure to account for the width of your insertion material if you're working with a pattern that is already meant to fit. In this case, half of that total width will need to be subtracted from the edge of the pattern pieces on both sides, or cut away from the edges of the existing garment panels.

Suggested Materials

Pins

Needle

Thread

Wax (if desired)

Thimble

Scissors

(continued)

The Resizing Method (Continued)

Resizing Method Steps

1. Begin by thread marking your stitching lines, as you'll be working from the right side of your garment and these lines will need to be visible from both sides. (See thread marking [page 30] for tips on this, if needed.)

2. Working from the right side of your garment, begin stitching the insertion lace to the first half of the fabric along your stitching line. This may be done by hand or by machine as you prefer. I personally like to use a combination stitch (page 61) for this, as insertion lace strips can be quite long and this method allows for both speed as well as the bit of strength provided by the intermittent backstitch. Note that a contrasting thread is used in this example for visibility, but the thread is usually chosen to match; otherwise, a running (page 55), back- (page 59) or half backstitch (page 60) may be preferred as the combination stitch is not the most visually pleasing.

3. Proceed to attach the second half of the fabric to the opposite edge of the lace in the same manner of stitching as you did for the first half.

4. The seam allowance is pressed back against the ground fabric, away from the insertion, and finished as you prefer (whether by overlocking, overcasting [page 79], pinking [page 76], turning and felling [page 85] or simply left raw). These seam allowances are then tacked back immediately—once again using the method of your preference—next to the edge of the insertion. This example uses a running stitch for speed as this is not a structural seam.

Pin Tucks

Otherwise known in the 19th century as simply "tucks," these can be used for decorative purposes or, practically, to reduce width or length in a garment, such as in children's clothing or garments that need to have adjustable room; simply remove the tucks as additional length or width is needed.

Tucks are fairly straightforward in their stitching, but the calculation of fabric to be added for tuck room can slightly complicate this process. To calculate the amount of fabric you will need for pin tucks, you will first need to know how many tucks you wish to add, and what width you wish your tucks to be. You will then have to double the width of the tuck, and multiply this doubled width by the number of tucks you plan to add.

Tucks are most easily and neatly achieved when worked on the straight grain of a plain-woven material, or the grain that runs parallel to the selvedge. While it's possible to work tucks on the cross grain or on the bias, this will require much more measurement and precision in handling to ensure that the fabric sits neatly and does not warp or stretch.

Tucks may be hand or machine stitched according to time and preference. If stitching by hand, it's often best to use a running stitch since these seams are usually many and aren't normally structural, so speed is preferable over strength. Sewing instructor Agnes Walker confirmed in 1907 that tucks are to be made with running stitches, and that backstitching these is "a waste of time and eyesight if done by hand."[13]

(continued)

Suggested Materials

Ruler

Marking tool (pencil, chalk or disappearing ink [optional])

Needle

Thread

Wax (if desired)

Thimble

Scissors

Iron

Pin Tucks (Continued)

Steps

1. To work tucks into your fabric, first measure out your tuck widths and spacing distances. So, for example, if you wish to add four ¼-inch (6-mm)-wide tucks to the center front of a blouse, you would double the width of each tuck to get ½ inch (1.3 cm), then multiply that by the four total tucks you want to put into the garment. Then—because fabric has a thickness and some width will be needed for the fabric to fold into the tuck, add an additional ⅛ inch or so (2 to 3 mm) per tuck, depending on the thickness of your material. This means that you will need to add 2 inches (4 cm) plus the additional ½ inch (1.3 cm) of fold ease to your pattern piece or fabric so as to accommodate the tucks.

2. Although it may be tempting to score lines or mark with dots down your fabric, I would not suggest doing this unless you're using disappearing marking pens, as tucks will need to be stitched from the right side of the garment. This isn't to say that extant garments containing stitched-over marking lines don't exist—they certainly do, sometimes in ink! However, I find it more neat and effective simply to pinch the two marks together at one end, then follow the grain of the fabric by eye across the length of the material, pressing a fold into it with my fingers.

3. Agnes Walker advised basting the tuck into place before stitching, which will be more necessary for hand-stitched tucks as you won't be able to use a sewing machine foot to gauge the distance of the stitching line from the edge of the tuck. The basting is worked ⅛ inch or less (1 to 3 mm) into the tuck so that the basting thread is not caught when the stitching line is worked.

4. When the tucks have been stitched, they're then pressed flat to one side according to preference.

Tip:

Whether or not this is your first time stitching tucks, it is usually best to do a sample on a bit of scrap material first before working them into your final garment. This will allow you to experiment with tuck width and the spacing between tucks to figure out which combination you think looks best according to your fabric choice and garment shape.

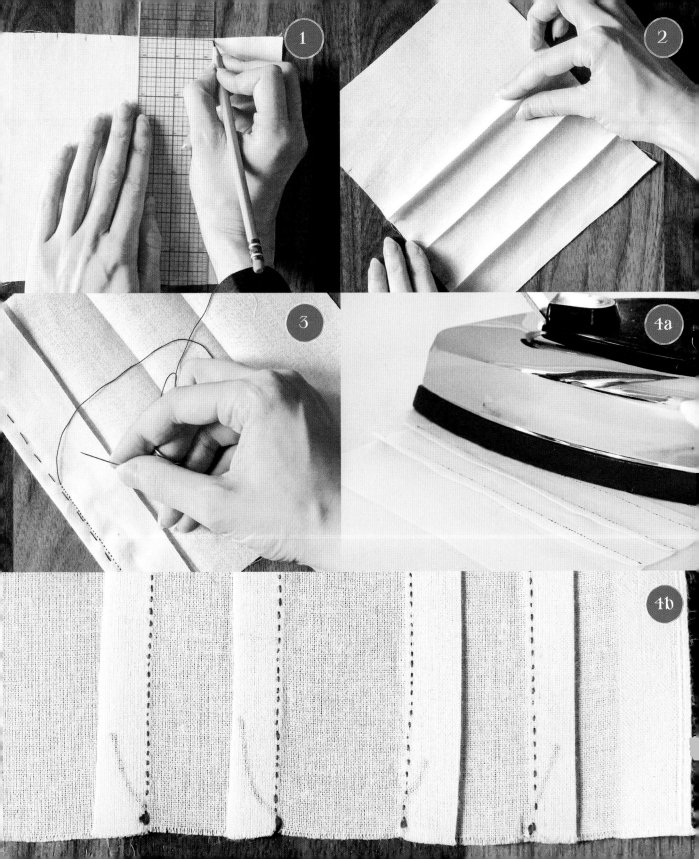

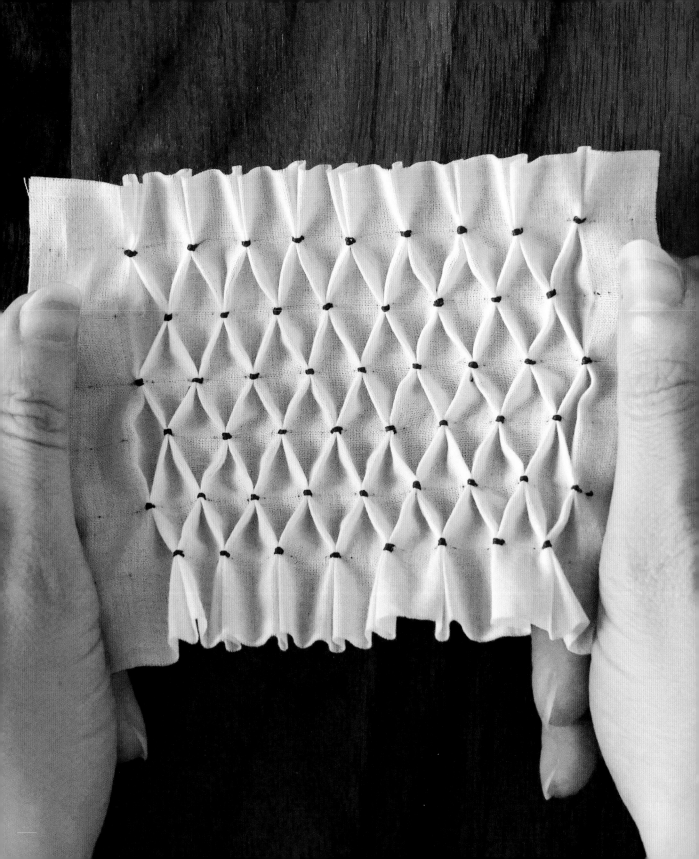

Smocking

Smocking, while highly decorative, also provides the practical benefit of allowing a close fit while maintaining a bit of elasticity, as a finished smocked portion of a garment will have a certain degree of stretch. There are infinite varieties of smocking design according to where the tacking stitches are placed as well as the initial pattern of the gathering threads, but we will start here with a simple smocking pattern alternately known in the late 19th century as honeycombing.[14]

The stretch ability is formed not through elasticity in any of the materials, but in the gathering of a longer length of material into a smaller space. A smocked section will therefore need to be at least two if not two and a half or three times the desired finished length, depending on the smocking design; this honeycombing method should require only a double length, but more complex smocking patterns that require the pleats to be stitched more closely together may require tripling.

(continued)

Suggested Materials

Ruler

Marking tool
(pencil, chalk or
disappearing ink)

Needle

Thread

Wax (if desired)

Thimble

Scissors

Smocking (Continued)

Steps

1. On the wrong side of your material, begin by scoring a series of horizontal rules across the length. The spacing of these is up to you and will dictate the size of your finished honeycombing, but this example uses ½-inch (1.3-cm) spacing per contemporary 19th-century instructions.

2. You'll then need to mark a series of dashes along your horizontal rules to mark your stitching points. The spacing of these should be the same as the distance of your horizontal rows, so in this example the dash marks are made ½ inch (1.3 cm) apart. Be sure that your dashes are perfectly vertically aligned.

3. Next, work your preliminary gathering threads along your horizontal rows, with each stitch measuring half the length of each square. This should be done with running stitches (page 55), and the thread should not be anchored at the start or finish.

4. The entry and exit points of the running stitches should align perfectly from one row to the next, similarly to the technique of cartridge pleating (page 132).

5. These gathering threads are then drawn up to form a series of uniform folds.

6. Anchor a thread on the wrong side of the material, then flip the work to the right side and take your first stitch at the peak of the first two folds at the first row, drawing the folds together. Take two or three stitches in place here to thicken the stitch for a more decorative appearance, especially if you're using a contrasting thread.

7. Your needle will then need to travel underneath the work, diagonally down to the second row, and exiting at the third fold.

8. Tack the second and third folds together, taking a couple of stitches in place to bulk up the stitch if desired.

9. Bring the needle under and back up to the first row at the third and fourth folds.

10. These are then drawn together in the same manner as the first two stitches. This completes the pattern that you will need to repeat along this first row.

11. Continue working in this zigzag pattern along the first two rows. When you've reached the end, you may remove the gathering threads to reveal your finished smocking design.

12. Repeat this process along the next pair of rows and down the remainder of your garment, working the rows in pairs and continuing your smocking pattern.

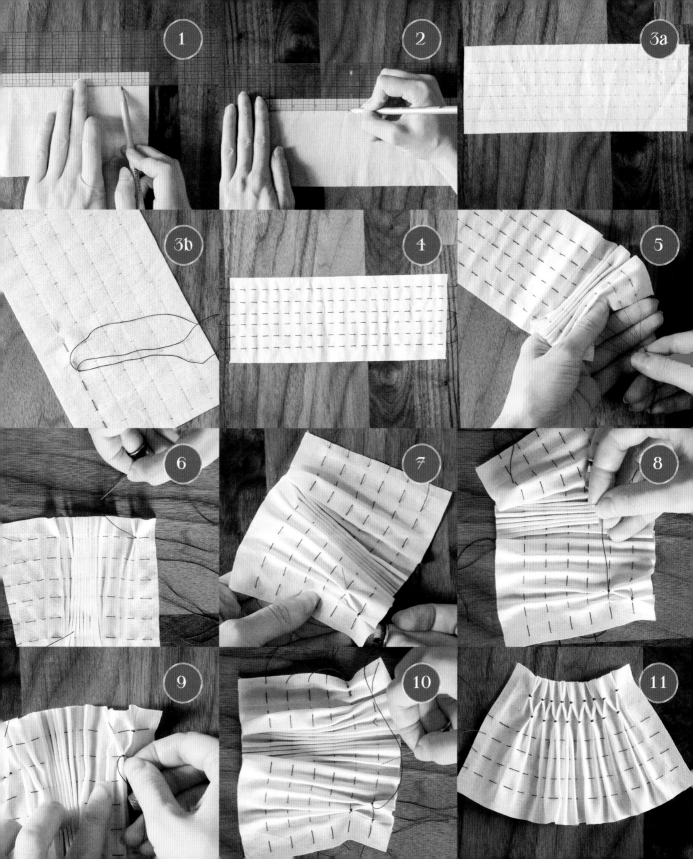

Feature: Sophia Khan

I grew up around old things. When I was young, my parents had a vintage furniture store. We would go to antique malls, flea markets, garage sales and even dumpster dive at times, much to my embarrassment. I always had the thrill of finding things when I was out hunting with them. While I was growing up, all the women in my immediate family knew how to sew and I quickly learned when I was still in the single digits. By the time I was in high school, I was making clothes for myself and friends and costumes for our drama program. When I was 16, I went to Chicago to do a summer fashion program. This is where I learned that fashion and making clothing could become a profession. I was obsessed with going to thrift stores and repurposing items into clothing and accessories in any way I could.

When I went to college for fashion design, I fell in love with all the avant-garde designers that we were told were the pinnacles of design. Costume and fashion were separated; we were taught that fashion shouldn't be costume. I remember firmly believing in this ideal. After that, I started working in the ready-to-wear fashion industry. I still loved vintage, but it had taken a backseat, though I would occasionally find some 1940s or '50s pieces to wear. When I started to dabble in pre-20th-century clothing, I made a pair of poly taffeta stays that I bound in lining fabric. They were not beautiful and did not fit well, but I was hooked. I wanted to make more and more historical items. Finding a community on the Internet helped me meet other people who made costume as clothing. After thinking for so long of costume as something that could be worn only on film or stage, I realized I could make costumes for myself just for the enjoyment of it.

Then, the collecting bug I was raised with bit me again. I was in a Brooklyn thrift store and found an Edwardian bodice for $3! It was hanging among the T-shirts and I just couldn't believe it. As I kept delving deeper into historical fashion, I kept finding neglected and often unwearable garments. I wanted to rescue them all and keep them from being thrown away. Friends started giving me garments that belonged to their great-grandparents and beyond. Studying these garments was a great way to improve my skills. I started to emulate the stitches I saw and find old sewing manuals to identify them. As I was improving my own sewing craft, I shifted careers and found myself working in costume departments instead of fashion. This was a better fit for me, as it wasn't trend-driven and I was making clothing for a more diverse group of people. By sewing my own clothing, I never had to worry about clothes fitting properly. I tend to be in the so-called midsized range where it can be difficult to find off-the-rack clothing that fits well. Nowadays, I find myself mixing vintage, contemporary and historical styles. Edwardian, art deco and 1960s fashions are some of my favorites. I'm not a purist and prefer to be eclectic. Through this journey with clothing, I learned that costume can be clothing and can be made by anyone.

—Sophia Khan (she/her)

Practical Alterations

Now that we have an understanding of the basic stitches and where to use them, we can go ahead and put our new skills to use in the form of some practical alterations. In knowing these basic stitching techniques and in having the confidence in your skill to be able to undertake an alteration project, you'll have a substantial advantage when hunting for unique new finds in secondhand shops where garments tend to be available in only one size. Your world of clothing options will open up tremendously if you're properly equipped to take on a bit of needlework. Hems can be shortened or lengthened (to an extent), seams can be unpicked and reshaped, insertion panels can be added to give you a bit more room wherever you might need it. I always like to remember that, fundamentally, a garment is just a bunch of pattern pieces. These can be reverted to their 2-D form and remade to fit your body specifically, may be traced and scaled up or down to make a whole new garment—or just pinched and adjusted here and there to make an already-great garment fit *just right.* Fit is, after all, where the secret magic to a truly extraordinary garment lies, and having the ability to take the fit of your clothes into your own hands is an invaluable skill.

If you've landed on this chapter before reading the previous section on basic stitching techniques, you may wish to use that chapter for reference as the individual steps of each stitch will not be explained in detail here.

Rehemming

This is a basic strategy for putting a hem into any garment, whether that is to shorten a pair of trousers, a skirt, a shirt, a dress, etc. The following example will be demonstrated on a pair of trousers, but feel free to adapt this method to the garment of your choice.

Suggested
Materials

Garment needing
a hem

Needle

Thread

Wax (if desired)

Thimble

Pins

Scissors

(continued)

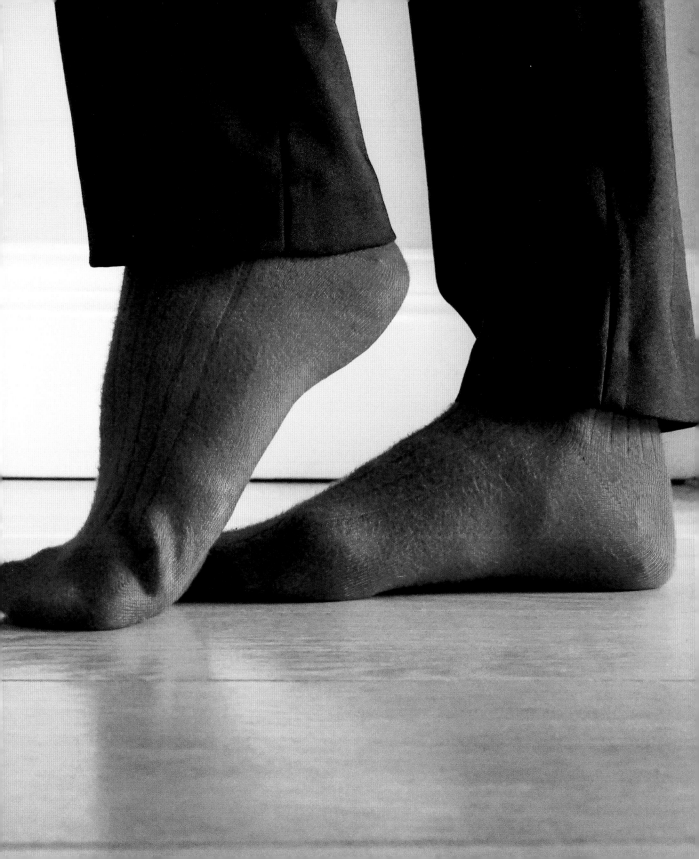

Rehemming (Continued)

Steps

1. Begin by putting on the garment to determine how much length will need to be subtracted. This can be done on trousers by roughly folding up and pinning the additional length until you reach the desired new height. It's best to have someone else do this for you so that you can concentrate your full efforts on standing as straightly as possible. If you must do this yourself, try to avoid bending your knees as much as possible, and always be sure to stand up straight and check the length and evenness of the new hem in a mirror before removing the trousers for alteration.

2. To mark an even hem on a skirt, this may be done in several ways: either by using a specially designed hem marker, which will spray chalk dust markings onto your garment at the set hem height; or in the more DIY fashion by taping a marker to a yard or meter stick at the desired height up from the floor and using that to mark the line onto your garment. Alternatively, a length of string may be taped between a doorway at your desired hem height, the string coated in chalk or charcoal dust, and then carefully pressed around the hem of the skirt to mark a rough line.

3. If the amount you're taking up in your hem is small (1 inch [2.5 cm] or less), you can get away with simply turning up the original finished hem and securing that down. If you need to take up a substantial amount of length, you'll need to cut away some of the existing length so as to get your new hem allowance to lay smoothly. If you're cutting a new raw edge, this will need to be finished off before stitching down: either by pressing it inward before the new hem is turned (as shown), or by stitching a strip of binding or seam tape to the right side

of the cuff a small ways in from the raw edge so that the hem can be turned up and the opposite edge of the binding secured to the inside. This latter option is slightly more time-consuming, especially if done by hand, but will produce a flatter seam.

4. The new hem is then secured to the inside of the garment using the method of your choice. This example is worked with a felling stitch (page 63), but a herringbone stitch (page 66) may also be used, unless the binding method has already been employed in the previous step. I would not recommend using a running stitch or backstitch for this step, as this will show through more prominently to the right side of the leg.

5. If your garment has a lining or facing, be sure only to catch the lining layer of material, so that no stitches will be seen from the right side; if your garment is single layer only, do your best to pick up the smallest amount of ground fabric as possible so that the stitches remain discreet.

Note:

Contrasting thread is used in this example for visibility, but thread should be matched when possible unless used for intentionally decorative purposes.

It is also often possible to lengthen a hem since a relatively wide seam allowance is usually left in, especially in trousers. This may be unpicked and re-stitched at a smaller seam allowance, giving a bit more room in the length, although the amount you're able to lengthen the garment will be determined by the amount of seam allowance left in a garment, so do be sure to check this before purchasing.

Adding Gussets to Sleeves

Modern clothing manufacturers have a habit of cutting large armholes in an effort to accommodate as many different body shapes into a single standard size as possible, but this can cause a whole host of problems for anyone who doesn't conform closely to those standard sizes. If you've ever had a shirt or jacket prevent you from raising your arms—or in which you can raise your arms only at the expense of pulling up the whole garment—rather than sizing down and dealing with inconvenient tightness in other areas, it might be time to think about adding a gusset.

A gusset is a small fabric insert that effectively closes in the depth of the armhole so that the body of the garment comes up closer to the armpit. The higher the point of connection between the sleeve and the garment body, the higher you will be able to lift your arms without pulling up your entire shirt or jacket, as your sleeve won't be pinning you down.

(continued)

Suggested Materials

Garment needing alteration

Pins

Seam ripper or thread snips

Scrap muslin (calico)

Marking tool (pencil, chalk or disappearing ink)

Fabric scissors

Matching fabric

Needle

Thread

Wax (if desired)

Thimble

Gusset inserted into the sleeve of a woman's linen shift; mid-19th century, made with mid-18th-century cutting and stitching practices

The difference in arm movement without vs with a gusset

Adding Gussets to Sleeves (Continued)

Pattern tip:

If you're making a garment from scratch, working with a pattern you have drafted yourself or a commercial pattern, you can actually be preemptive about gussets by working the additional room into the sleeve pattern itself, saving yourself the visible seams. The scoop taken at the underarm point of a sleeve pattern will dictate the depth of the armhole: If this is scooped very low and you know you generally have problems moving your arms in garments, then you might wish to smooth out that curve a bit in advance to add a couple of inches (2.5 to 5 cm) between your arm and body.

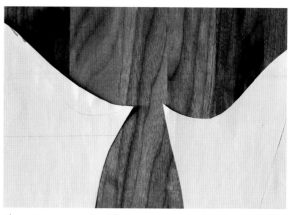

Two sleeve patterns: The pattern on the left has included the gusset shape into the arm scoop, whereas the pattern on the right has not.

Steps

1. To add a gusset to your garment, first put it on to determine where the gusset will need to go, and mark these points with pins. These points generally should not extend past the teres major and minor muscles that connect the arm and form the armpit, so the gusset won't be visible when the arms are lowered.

2. Using a seam ripper or embroidery snips, carefully split the seam between your pins to detach the bottom of the sleeve from the body of the garment.

3. For this next step, you will need a square of muslin (calico in the UK and parts of Europe) or other scrap cloth that is long enough to cover the length of your split seam. Securely pin this scrap of material to the sleeve edge of the split seam.

4. This step is a little tricky, so it is best done with the assistance of another person, but is still possible to do on your own if you're careful. Raise your arm to see how much separation you'll need between your sleeve and the body of your garment: The muslin pinned to the sleeve should fill in the gap. Carefully place a pin into the lower seam edge to secure the lower armscye to the muslin. Don't worry about getting it absolutely smooth and perfect; this can be adjusted later, as long as you have the general distance needed.

5. It's best to try to get three pins into that lower edge: one in the center, at the side seam, and two on either side. These second two might not be easy to do neatly on your own, so don't worry if you're not able to place these.

6. Once your garment is removed from your body, you can go in and adjust your pins so that the muslin shape sits smoothly between the sleeve and the body.

(continued)

Adding Gussets to Sleeves
(Continued)

7. Before removing your pins, trace around the edge of your shape on the muslin. Be sure to trace at the *stitching line*, where the seam will need to be stitched, not at the direct edge of the fabric.

8. Be sure also to mark any reference points to help you insert the gusset later: The side seam of your garment, the underseam of your sleeve, and which edge should connect to the sleeve vs the body are usually useful points to have.

9. Now your pattern shape can be unpinned and cut out along your traced line to give you your gusset pattern. You could trace this onto paper if you'd like, but personally I don't see much point in this since these gusset pieces are usually individual to the needs of each alteration and aren't easily reused.

10. Cut out your gusset pieces from the fabric of your choice, ensuring that you leave yourself some seam allowance if this was not included in your pattern. When marking, be sure to transfer any balance marks to your fabric. Ideally the fabric used should match the garment as closely as possible. Plain colors should be easy to find in your local fabric store, but prints may be more difficult to match. Is there a lining or facing in your garment, a bit of hem that you can shorten or that will be tucked into a waistband and won't be seen, that you might be able to borrow for gusset material? If not, try to match the fabric as closely as possible. Note: The fabric used for this example is contrasted deliberately for ease of visibility.

11. Your gusset piece can then be pinned into the garment, aligning the gusset according to your balance marks and orientation notes.

12. Proceed to stitch the gusset into place. This may be done by hand or by machine per your preference. If stitching by hand, I would recommend using a firm backstitch (page 59) as armscye seams tend to take a lot of strain.

13. The edges may then also be finished according to your preference. Once again, I would recommend using as firm a finishing method as possible (overlocking, turning and felling (page 85) or binding (page 80) are your best options) as these seams come into heavy contact with the body.

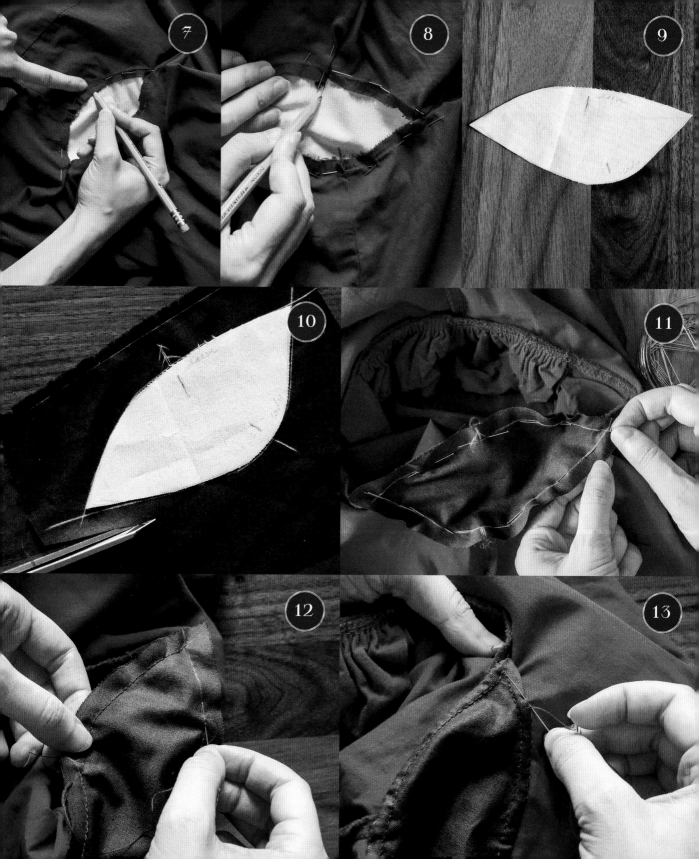

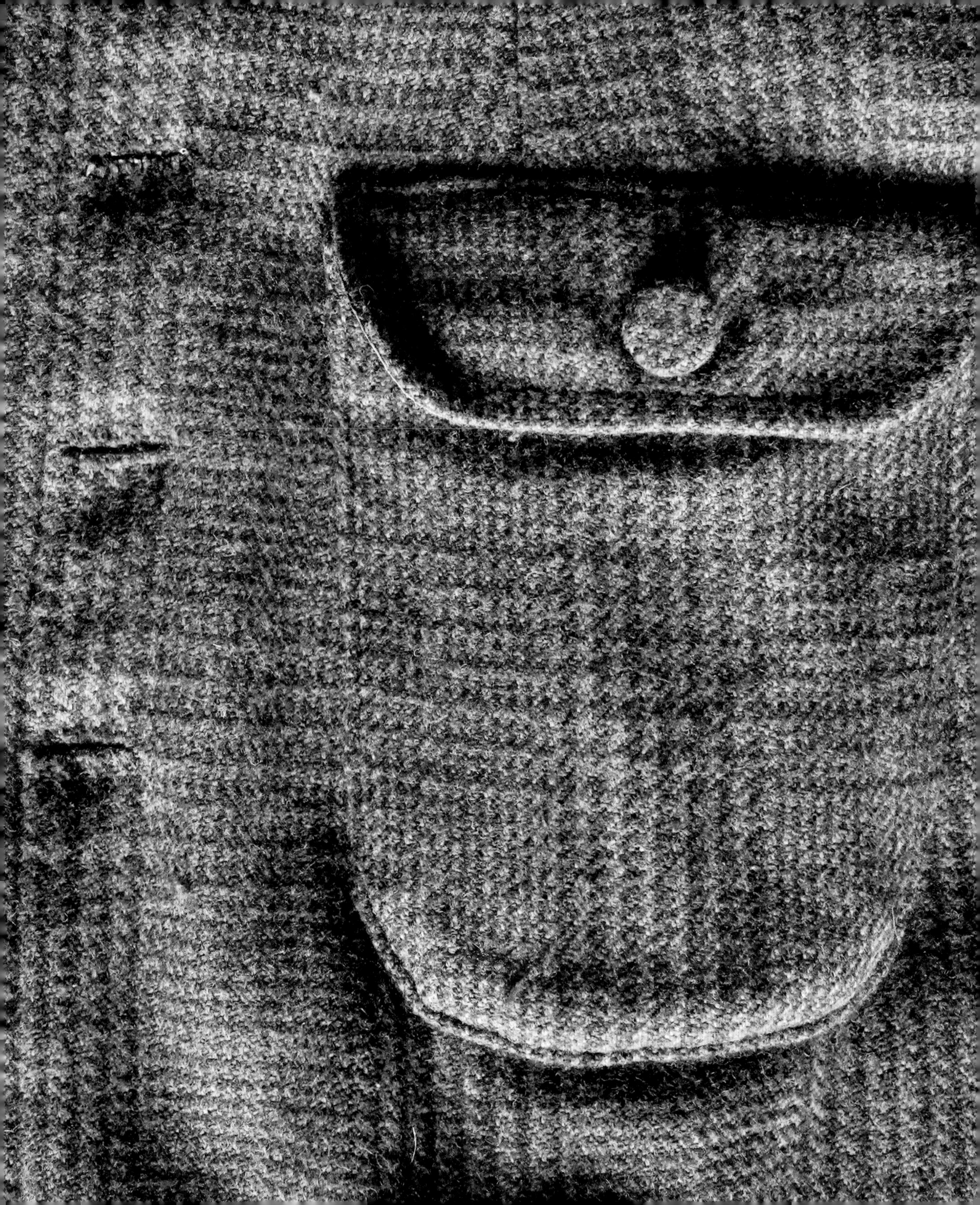

Adding Pockets

Pockets: a feat of human invention that modern fashion for some reason often wishes to do away with. But fear not, for pockets are very easy to add to most garments and can be done in as little as an hour—even by hand.

Patch Pockets

This style of pocket does not involve splitting or cutting a seam into your garment, but makes a pocket that sits on top of the existing fabric. This may be preferable if you don't wish to structurally change the garment or if you think you might want to remove or reposition the pocket later. Patch pockets may be made in matching or contrasting fabric, they may sit on the outside of the garment or on the inside to provide some secret storage room for change, cards, a phone, a watch or any such items one desires to keep close.

Symmetry tip:

To draft perfectly symmetrical shapes quickly, measure and draw only one half of your intended shape. For example, I've only drawn the curve on half of the bottom of my pocket shape; when cutting, I'll fold the paper along my marked halfway points and cut double so that when unfolded, each half is exactly the same as the other.

Suggested Materials

Ruler

French curve (or other rounded object to trace curves around)

Sturdy or tightly woven fabric for the pockets

Marking tool (pencil, chalk or disappearing ink)

Pins

Fabric scissors

Iron (optional)

Needle

Thread (strong thread recommended)

Wax (if desired)

Thimble

Seam ripper or thread snips

Measuring tape

(continued)

Patch Pockets (Continued)

Steps

1. Begin by determining the size and shape of your pocket. These can be squared, rounded, pointed—or any shape, really. Just be sure that it's large enough to hold your planned items.

2. A ruler will be helpful for drafting straight lines, and a French curve will assist in drawing smooth curves if you've incorporated those into your pocket design.

3. If you wish to add a flap to your pocket so that it may button shut, you also may need to draw this onto your pattern—especially if you plan to add any decorative shaping to the flap edge.

4. Your pocket pieces may then be cut from whatever fabric you wish. If your pocket fabric is not sturdy enough on its own, you may need to cut a second piece from an interfacing or stiffer material to interline your pocket so that it will be strong enough to hold your items. You might also wish to cut a lining to seal off raw edges or to smooth the inside of the pocket, but this is up to you. This example is cut from a silk taffeta, which will be strong enough to hold a watch or some change as intended.

5. The seam allowance edges around your pocket will need to be folded in, and I've pressed these so that the pocket shape will be easier to work with. If your pocket involves any curved edges, these may need to be clipped intermittently so that the allowances can fold easily around the curves. When clipping seam allowances, do not clip past your stitching line into your pattern shape.

6. The pocket shape is then positioned where you'd like it to sit, and may be pinned or basted into place temporarily.

7. After beginning your stitch at one of the opening edges of your pocket, take a couple of strong backstitches (page 59) in place to firmly secure this corner to the ground fabric. These points will need to take a lot of strain, as they'll be pulled slightly every time items are inserted into the pocket, so be sure that these are nice and strong.

8. Proceed to stitch around the perimeter of your pocket shape, excluding the opening edge. It's up to you whether you wish to work by hand or by machine, and which stitch you choose to use—although inside pockets will need to be done by hand so that the stitching doesn't show through to the right side of the garment, unless your pocket can be sewn into the lining piece before it's made up into a garment, in which case it may be put in by machine. This example uses a hand-worked backstitch in strong silk thread, but this can also be worked with a felling stitch (page 63) if you'd like a less conspicuous stitching line.

9. The final stitch is once again worked with a series of backstitches in place to firmly secure it to the ground fabric.

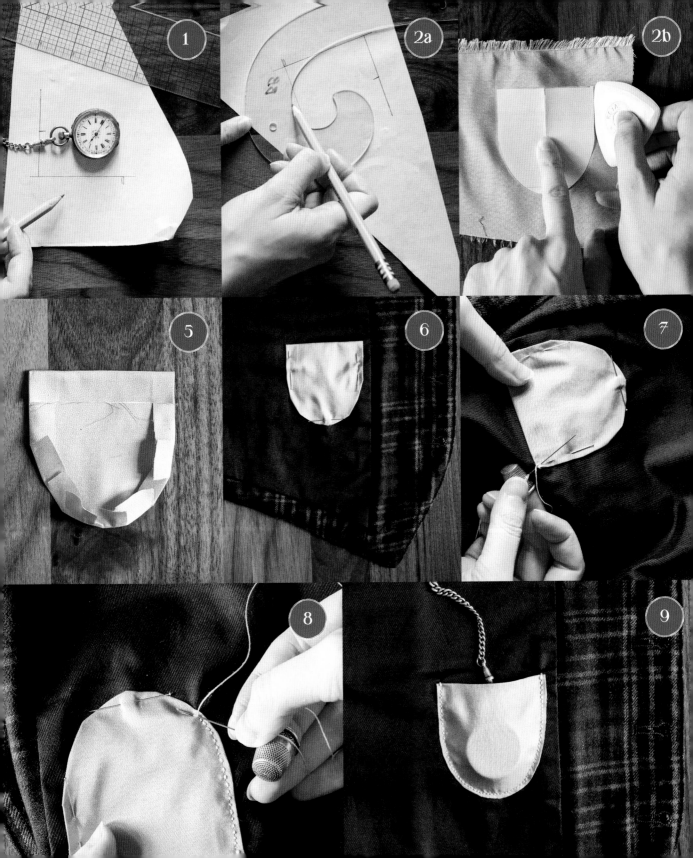

Seam Pockets

This style of pocket will sit in an existing seam or cut slit in a garment and is preferable for pockets that you wish to remain concealed.

Steps (See photos on pages 167 and 168)

Steps (See photos on pages 167 and 168)

1. Begin by determining where you'd like your pocket to sit. On lower garments, it should sit high enough to be easily reached with the hand. If you are making a loose skirt and have wide hips, you may wish to place this just below the fullest part of the hips so as not to add width, unless that's what you fancy. Place a pin into the seam where you want the top of your pocket to start.

2. Time for a little pattern drafting; I promise this will be easy! While you can certainly just draw your pocket pieces straight onto the fabric, it's much handier to have a trusty pocket shape on paper that you can reuse for future pocketing endeavors.

3. You'll need two very important measurements, the first being the width of the pocket opening, which should be wide enough to fit your hand comfortably, plus a little bit of extra room. This opening edge should be perfectly straight and should be cut on the straight of grain.

(continued)

Suggested Materials

Pins

Ruler

French curve (or other rounded object to trace curves around)

Marking tool (pencil, chalk or disappearing ink)

Sturdy or tightly woven fabric for the pockets

Fabric scissors

Seam ripper or thread snips

Needle

Thread (strong thread recommended)

Wax (if desired)

Thimble

Iron

Measuring tape

Seam Pockets (Continued)

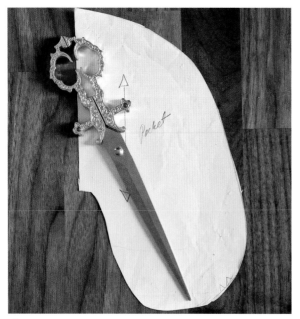

This pair of scissors would not be very secure in this pocket shape.

4. The second measurement you'll need is the depth from the bottom of the pocket opening to the bottom of the pocket bag. This should be low enough to cradle whatever you plan to be carrying in your pocket. Keep in mind that any part of an object extending above that pocket opening line will be prone to falling out, so make this as deep and wide as you need it to be.

5. Once you have your pattern piece, cut out two mirrored pieces from the pocket fabric of your choice. Be sure to add seam allowance if you didn't include this in your pattern.

6. On your garment, locate the pin you marked earlier.

7. Turning your garment inside out and transferring your top pin mark so that it's visible from the inside, proceed to measure down the length of your pocket opening (or lay your pocket piece with the top starting at the marking pin so that the edge of the pocket opening aligns with the seam edge) and place a pin to mark the bottom point of the pocket opening.

8. Carefully clip the stitching in your garment seam between these two marked points to reveal an opening space for your pocket. It's okay if you go a little distance (up to ½ inch [2.5 cm]) past these markings; this extra space will give you a bit more wiggle room and can be easily closed up later.

(continued)

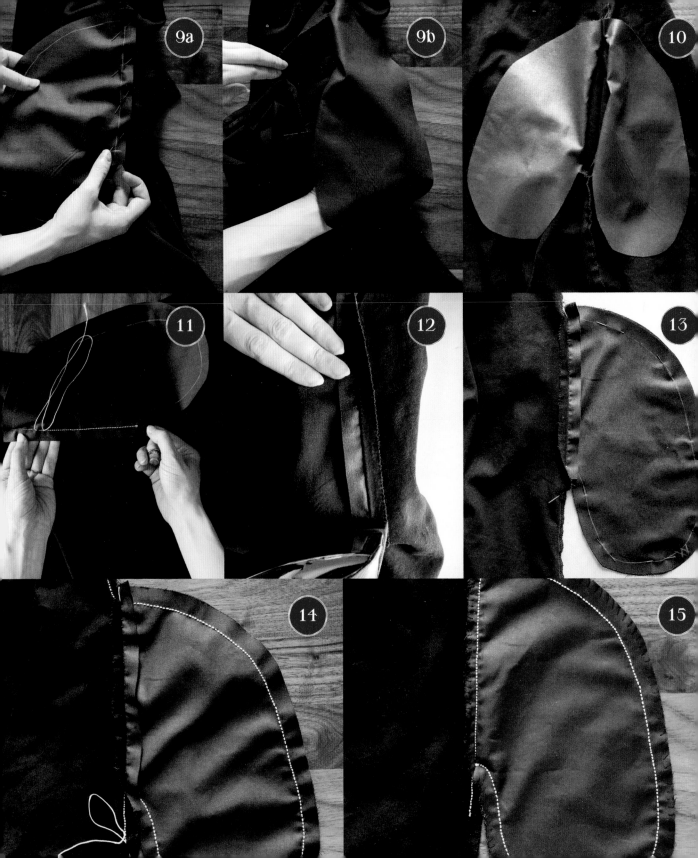

Seam Pockets (Continued)

9. Still working with your garment inside out, align one of your pocket pieces so that the edge of the pocket opening matches with the split in the garment seam. The "inside" face of the pocket piece (i.e., the piece that you will be able to feel when you put your hand inside) should be facing the outside of your garment so that your stitching lines are visible and your raw edges will face the inside of the garment. Pin this piece in place along the opening edge.

10. Repeat this pinning process for the second half of the pocket, making sure that the top edges of your pocket shapes align perfectly at the top of the opening. (You may have some extra room at the top and bottom of your split seam; this is perfectly fine and will be easy to close later, but just make sure your pocket pieces aren't slightly skewed.)

11. Begin stitching each half of the pocket to the garment seam along the opening edge. This can be done using the method of your choice, either by machine or by hand. This example uses a backstitch (page 59), which is recommended if the pocket is expected to hold heavy objects. (Note that the stitching in this example is done in contrasting thread for ease of visibility, but may be done in matching thread for a less conspicuous look.)

12. Both of these seams are then pressed open to crease the pocket seam.

13. You may then align both of the extending pocket shapes and pin them together along the stitching line. If you added balance marks to your pattern, you may use these to ensure that your pocket shapes are perfectly aligned, although this is usually doable by eye if your shapes are small enough and your fabric is stable.

14. The pocket is then stitched together all around the pocket bag using the method of your choice. It is usually wise to begin a little ways above the pocket opening on the garment seam, travel down and around the pocket, then come back onto the seam and travel a little ways down the garment seam once again to close any additional opening space left as well as to secure any loose threads from the clipped seam. This example is once again done with a backstitch, although this is only necessary if your pocket is meant to hold heavy or pointed objects (such as keys or scissors), but may alternately be done a bit quicker by only backstitching the bottom portion of the pocket bag while running (page 55) or combination stitching (page 61) the upper half.

15. The raw edges of your pocket may be finished off using the method of your choice if your garment will be washed regularly or is made from a fray-prone fabric, although if your fabric is tightly woven and your garment has a lining that will protect the pocket from frequent contact, it may be fine with raw edges alone. This example has been overcast (page 79) at the edges as the fabric is fairly stable, but edges can alternatively be overlocked, turned and felled (page 85), pinked (page 76) or, for additional strength, may be bound (page 80).

Feature: Embry Whitmore

My name is Embry.

My name and sewing came into my life at the same time: I was feeling very unmoored, waiting for the gender-affirming chest reduction surgery that had gotten postponed due to COVID-19, and feeling that who I was as a person was on pause.

I began sewing to find a way to press the Play button and to free myself from that interminable sense of being stuck. Initially, that was my only goal: Make clothes designed for a flatter chest for future-Embry as a way to feel less trapped by my circumstances while waiting for my gender-affirming surgery.

But it turns out sewing is way, way more than a perfunctory way to clothe one's body. It's performance; I've always been a maker, and when I realized making clothing was no different than painting or writing, it felt like the entire world opened up for me.

Like many sewers, I became entranced with the historical garments of eras past. The delicate pin tucks of Victorian petticoats, the smooth and buttery wool of breeches, the insertion lace that took the Edwardian era by storm, the structure of a well-tailored waistcoat. . . . And re-creating them is enticing.

But more enticing? Making them with my own spin.

I am a nonbinary human. I was assigned female at birth and it doesn't suit me. But I'm not a man, either. I am trans, in the sense that I am transforming myself constantly. In the sense that I am transversing the gender experience. I live a fluid and an un-pin-downable gender experience, and I wouldn't have it any other way.

But what that means is that the corsetry and petticoats of traditional women's wear don't suit me—I feel trapped and claustrophobic in them, just like I felt trapped and claustrophobic in my presurgery body. It also means that breeches and waistcoats of traditional menswear don't suit me either. Historical clothing is fascinating and beautiful and enrapturing, but it is also rigidly gendered in a way that does not feel good on my body or soul. This is not how everyone who is nonbinary or trans feels, but it is very much how I experience things.

So, I began my current journey: embarking on a quest to make things that do feel good on my body and soul and are also inspired by historical garments.

That means shirts made of beautiful delicate cotton, cut in a "masculine" shape to not emphasize waist or chest, but with sleeves that are pin tucked and beautiful. It means a shirtwaist, cut out of silk and emphasizing wide powerful shoulders peppered with insertion lace. It means all the wonderful parts of both "masculine" and "feminine" clothing, forged together into something new. It means creating a new way to experience historically inspired costuming without submitting to gender binary.

And most important, it means feeling at home and comfortable in the things I make.

I started this journey alone and lonely, making things in solitude to help me through a transition period in my life. But not only have I learned how to make things I love, I've also found a beautiful community of fellow nonbinary and transgender makers. This world is full of people who also make things to feel at home in their bodies and in their communities. I feel lucky every day to count myself among them.

—Embry Whitmore (they/them)

Care and Feeding: Making Clothes Last

People who have plenty of money, and do not care to bother with clothes cleaning, can either give their old clothing away, or throw them away when they become soiled, but most people need to keep their clothes as long as there is substantial wear in them, and a big bill of expense is saved by knowing how to do the cleaning and pressing at home (*Home and Health*, 1907).[15]

The story is a bit different today, over 100 years later: One doesn't need plenty of money to opt to discard clothing that has been damaged or soiled rather than mending or cleaning instead. Clothing is abundant, mostly inexpensive, and it is much more time-efficient to simply stop teaching and learning the skills necessary to preserve and maintain our clothes. But this, as we know, comes with a steep ethical and environmental cost.

Late 19th- and early 20th-century home manuals and sewing guides are teeming with tips on mending techniques. These techniques aren't relegated to a separate chapter but are included with the stitching techniques themselves—such was the equal importance they had within a person's sewing knowledge. In fact, mending is arguably the most important aspect of sewing that the general clothes-wearer can know: If you're going to learn any sewing at all, starting with the essential skills to care for the clothes you already have is the best place to begin.

Prevention

Ideally, it is best to avoid the need for mending in the first place through carefully maintaining your clothes to the best of your ability. Regularly checking your clothing for thin patches or strained seams will allow you to fortify these weak spots before they become holes, and knowing when and how to wash is the first step toward preserving the durability of the materials.

I maintain the belief that the automatic washing machine is high up on the list of humankind's greatest inventions. Before we had the ability to merrily get on with our lives as a machine diligently scrubbed our clothes clean, laundry days—for those who couldn't afford to send the washing out—was an all-consuming event, beginning at the break of dawn and carrying on for the better part of the day. It required immense physical labor in the scrubbing, wringing or manual machine operation, and often meant a day of cold meals as the fires would be occupied with heating the water for laundering.[16] Washing was done when necessary, but it was certainly not a mindless or nondisruptive task.

Now that washing machines have taken much of the time, manual labor and stove occupation out of the equation, we have gotten ourselves into the habit of throwing *everything* in the wash all the time purely out of custom, regardless of whether a garment actually *needs* to be washed, much to the detriment of the fabrics that make up our clothes. Even worse, for stretch fibers especially, is the tumble dryer.

If we do choose to give a garment another wear or two before washing, we are often left in a state of indecision over what to do with it: It isn't dirty enough for the washing basket, but we are also under the assumption that it isn't clean enough to go back into the wardrobe, and so it's relegated to a place of purgatory (usually a chair). (Admit it. I know you have one, too.)

We often wonder why people throughout history bothered with—or tolerated—the practice of layering their clothes so extensively. Far from an obligation to strict societal expectation—or even willful oppression, according to some modern narratives—the act of layering one's clothing is actually a highly practical decision: By protecting the visible garments (which were often made from nicer materials, as these would be on view to the public) from contact with the body, these layers would be less susceptible to soiling and thus would not need to be washed except to be spot cleaned or aired when necessary. Underlayers would act as a barrier between the body and the outer layers of clothing. These were most often made from hard-wearing cottons and linens, cellulose fibers that not only can withstand frequent and vigorous washing but that are also naturally inclined to absorb moisture, keeping the body clean and dry during wear. One then needed only to change out one's underlayers daily to be able to rewear the outer layers—shockingly to our modern habits—multiple days in the week.

Departing momentarily from history for tips on washing practices, the worlds of theatre and film costume have some additional tips to help us keep our clothes fresh between washes:

These performance garments, often made from specialty materials, are danced and moved in, heavily sweated in, and sometimes need to be worn for long hours or donned twice in a day, and so need to be kept clean and fresh at a moment's notice.

Vodka spray: Lightly spritzing the inside of your garment with a spray bottle filled with clear alcohol will kill odor-causing bacteria and can be used safely on most fabrics. This will dry clear and quickly, unless the alcohol has been mixed with some water, in which case drying time may be slightly extended. Do not try this on fine silks, as the liquid may leave behind staining, especially if the mixture has been diluted.

Airing: Turning a garment inside out and giving it some air flow will help dry garments quickly and prevent odor. For the best results, a garment should be hung outside or in front of a fan. Bonus points if you're able to hang the garment in direct sunlight to take additional advantage of the germicidal properties of the sun's UV rays.

Removable linings: Taking a page from historical sartorial habit, some costumes with more complex and nonwashable exteriors are constructed with washable underlayers that snap, tie or are loosely stitched in and that can be removed for easy washing, while the rest of the costume remains out of direct contact with the body. This saves the actor from having to put on additional layers of clothing as would have been done historically, as these layers are already built into the garment itself.

Removable underarm shields are also available for purchase (or are very simple to make), and can be extremely useful in protecting the underarms of your garment from skin contact. These can be swapped out and washed as needed, while the garment itself stays clean for multiple wears.

Hand washing clothes is also an excellent alternative to the washing machine. While many washing machines today have delicate or hand wash cycles and so are not as destructive to the clothes as they once were, garments in need of a quick interim wash between full loads of machine washing can easily be done by hand. It is best to avoid the dryer whenever possible, though: Air drying will significantly prolong the life of your garments (particularly those containing any element of elastic or stretch).

What to Do About Shoes?

While shoemaking and thus shoe repair requires tools, skill and hand strength beyond the average craftsperson, shoe maintenance is still something that we should—but often don't—think about. It's *really* difficult to completely destroy a good pair of shoes—and it's still mildly difficult to wear out even a cheap pair of shoes—if you have a good cobbler on hand. Soles can be replaced and refastened, scuffs can be repaired, so it's worth finding a cobbler in your area who will be able to take care of your shoes whenever they need some attention. Good-quality leather shoes will last you for decades and can withstand much more abuse with fewer repairs. Unfortunately though, as of now, synthetic leathers are not as durable and will wear out quicker; the extensive and frequent repairs often needed for less-durable shoes may cost just as much if not more than a cheap new pair of faux-leather shoes, fueling the temptation to simply purchase new shoes and throw away the old ones.

Mending

All the prevention efforts in the world still won't defeat the occasional need for mending. Accidents happen—buttons come loose, fabrics snag or tear or simply wear out with day-to-day activity.

The good news is, unless your garment has been burned or otherwise wholly destroyed, virtually all damage is fixable.

Darning

The first rule of darning, according to sewing instructor Agnes Walker in 1907, is "Never wait for a hole."[17] *Darning can be both a preventative measure taken to strengthen areas on a garment that are beginning to wear thin in an effort to ward off a hole—or darning can be used to repair an area that we have, admittedly, let wear through into a full hole. It happens to the best of us.*

Steps

1. Begin by positioning your darning mushroom (or other smooth object of your choice) directly under the affected area.

2. Begin your thread, ensuring that the tail of the thread is left to the inside of your garment. The start of your thread should be positioned on a firm part of the material, not on any worn or thin patches, so that the entirety of these may be covered with reinforcement and the stress points of your darning patch will always fall on firm material.

3. Work a running stitch (page 55) from the bottom of your thinned patch, until you've passed the top of it and are once again on firm material.

4. Leaving a small loop at the top, bring your thread around and work a running stitch back downward, immediately next to your previous column of stitching. This loop on the end is essential, especially if your garment is made of stretch material. Having this extra slack in your darning rows will allow your garment to stretch nicely into shape and will give your patch a bit of room for when the wool shrinks up. Otherwise, your darned patch will pull and pucker against the material of your garment and potentially cause more tears.

Suggested Materials

Clothing to be darned

Some sort of smooth and slightly rounded object to work on, such as a purpose-made darning mushroom/ egg (which can be found relatively inexpensively on eBay or in your local craft shop, or alternatively a small mug, lightbulb, piece of firm produce or even a computer mouse will do just as well)

A thick tapestry needle (or any needle with an eye large enough to pass your thread or yarn through)

Darning thread or yarn (preferably wool)

(continued)

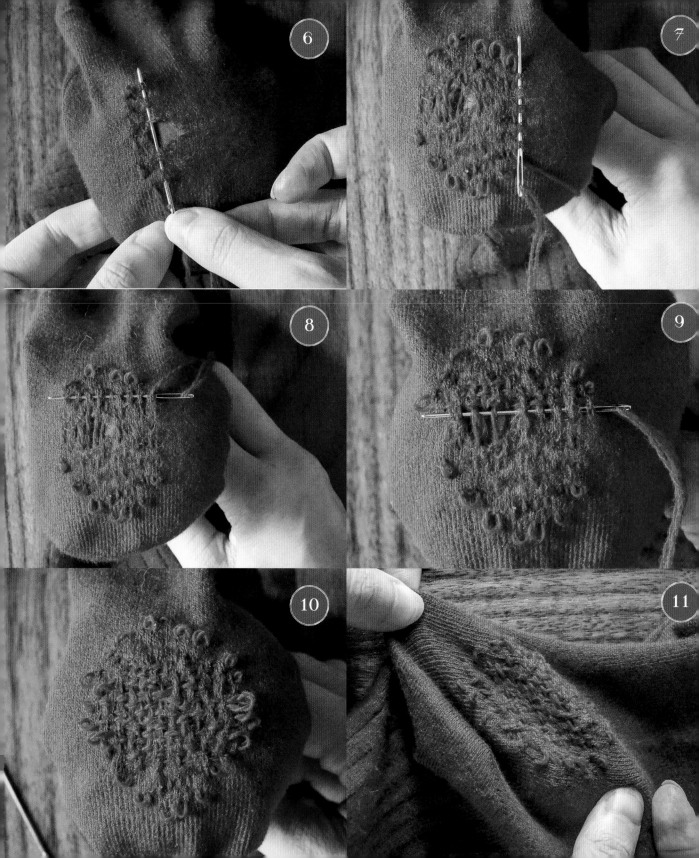

Darning (Continued)

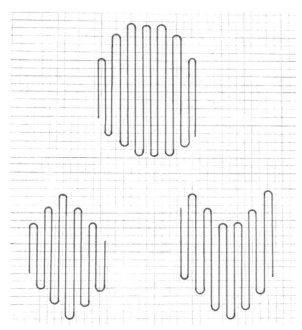

Darning patterns after diagram in Walker's 1907 manual

5. It is also important to ensure that you vary the heights at which the thread changes direction at the turning point of each row. Your threads should not form a perfectly square patch, but an irregular, circular or oval one, so that the tension points at the ends of your stitching will not all pull on the same threads of your ground material and cause a tear.

6. Continue your columns of running stitches, ensuring that you're leaving loops at the top and bottom when changing directions. When you reach a patch with a hole, simply stretch the thread across and continue your running stitch on the other side. Do not try to pull the threads together to close the hole.

7. These vertical rows should continue until all worn and thin patches are covered and firm material is reached again on the other side.

8. This process of running stitching is then continued horizontally, beginning once again from the topmost portion of your working area where the material has not been thinned. This time, however, the running stitches should be worked alternately over and under the vertical threads to form a weave.

9. When you reach the point of a worn hole, the horizontal threads can then be woven under and over your vertical threads to form a new expanse of material. These threads should be packed as tightly together as possible to encourage them to felt during wash and wear.

Tip:

If you run out of thread, you can finish off and restart a thread at the end of any of your rows.

10. Finish your horizontal stitches when you've reached a patch at the bottom that is no longer thin.

11. If your garment stretches, it may now be gently stretched a bit to work some of the loops into place, but don't worry if they don't all sort out immediately; the threads should shrink further when washed.

Patching

When a large hole has worn through your fabric or it's had the audacity to tear at a place that isn't a seam, then you may need to add a patch to repair the material. When making garments yourself, it's best to keep back a couple of scraps for this purpose; otherwise, you'll need to source some material to match your garment as closely as possible.

Suggested Materials

Scrap material to match
your garment, large
enough to generously
cover the hole

Scissors

Iron

Needle

Thread

Wax (if desired)

Thimble

Pins

Tip:

Sometimes you may be able to steal some of the same fabric from elsewhere on your garment. If, for example, there is a lining or facing that isn't seen, or if you've thrifted the garment and then resized or shortened it and saved the excess material, this can be perfect for patching. When patching a print, bonus points if you can find an area in the leftover material that perfectly matches the area to be patched. Note: If your patching fabric has not been prewashed, it may be best to run this through the wash once or twice; otherwise, your patch may shrink your garment when it's washed in the future.

Steps

1. Begin by cutting a patch piece that will generously cover the torn area, including a bit of seam allowance.

2. Press the edges of your patch piece inward to crease, then pin your patch over the affected area on the right side of your garment.

3. Baste (page 56) around the edges of your patch to hold it more firmly in place.

4. Work a felling stitch (page 63) around your patch to secure it. Note that this example uses a contrasting thread for visibility, but a matching thread can be used for a more discreet look unless you wish to show off your mending decoratively.

5. Once you have finished felling the front side, you may remove the basting stitches.

6. Flipping your piece over to the wrong side, cut four slits into the ground fabric at the corners, but do not cut all the way to the edge.

7. You may need to trim away a bit of width from these four edges of your ground fabric. More width will mean a thicker and more noticeable seam; less width will make for a finer seam but may be more tedious to handle.

8. Gently fold each side under to conceal the raw edge, then baste into place to secure temporarily. (Note: Basting may be replaced with pinning if you are in a hurry, but the pins will force the fabric to warp slightly and will make it more difficult to achieve neat and straight edges.)

9. Fell down the edges of this inner fold, then remove your basting stitches. Give your finished patch a good pressing to smooth things into shape.

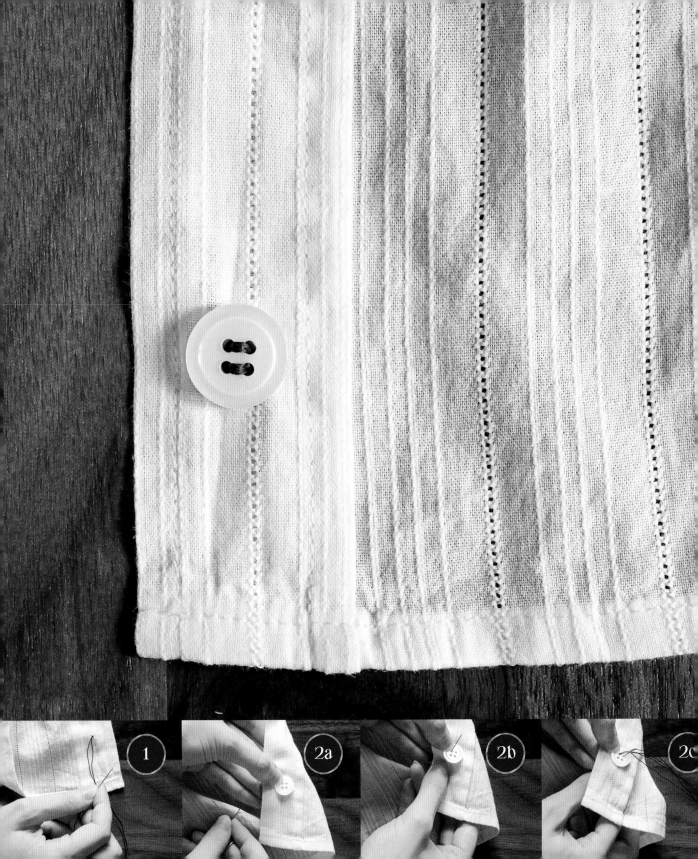

Reattaching Buttons

This is probably one of the most common clothing fixes out there, and a task most clothes wearers are faced with at some point in our clothes-wearing careers. Despite being an element of a garment designed to take significant strain, buttons are often very loosely attached and prone to coming undone quickly. Many a fast fashion blouse have I acquired in the past only to find its buttons so loosely attached that I proceeded to rip off and reattach the buttons more strongly myself as a preventative measure.

Flat Buttons

These are the most common style of button used in everyday clothing, and fortunately their reattaching is fairly straightforward and quick to do. Flat buttons may be made either with two holes or with four. This demonstration will be worked on a four-hole button to illustrate the additional step needed for the second set of holes.

Steps

1. Using a strong doubled thread, begin by anchoring your stitch (page 50) on the wrong side of the garment near the position you would like the button to sit, burying the tail of the thread between the two layers of material if possible.

Suggested Materials

Needle

Thread (strong thread such as buttonhole twist is recommended)

Wax (if desired)

Thimble

Buttons of your choosing

Scissors

2. Hold your button in position on the right side of the garment, ensuring that the button is rotated so that the holes are aligned straight up and down. Bring the needle up through one hole. It doesn't matter which hole you begin on or in which direction you stitch (whether left to right or up and down), as long as you repeat the same pattern for the second set of holes.

(continued)

Flat Buttons (Continued)

3. This example is working the stitch horizontally and from left to right, so the needle is brought down through the right hole of the top row and exits through the fabric onto the wrong side of the garment. Do *not* pull this thread too tightly—there should be 1 to 2 mm of ease between the button and the fabric.

4. Repeat the stitch along this first set of holes three or four times, ensuring that the thread is pulled uniformly and not too tightly.

5. Proceed to secure the second row of holes in the same manner as the first, working the stitch through the same number of times. This step is not necessary if your button only has one set of holes.

6. When you have finished securing the button and the needle is brought through to the wrong side of the garment, you'll then need to bring the needle back up to the right side of the garment *without* entering through any holes in the button.

7. Wrap your thread a couple of times around the base of the button to strengthen the post, or the space between the button and the ground fabric where the other half of your garment will sit. Tie off your thread by anchoring it on the wrong side of your garment.

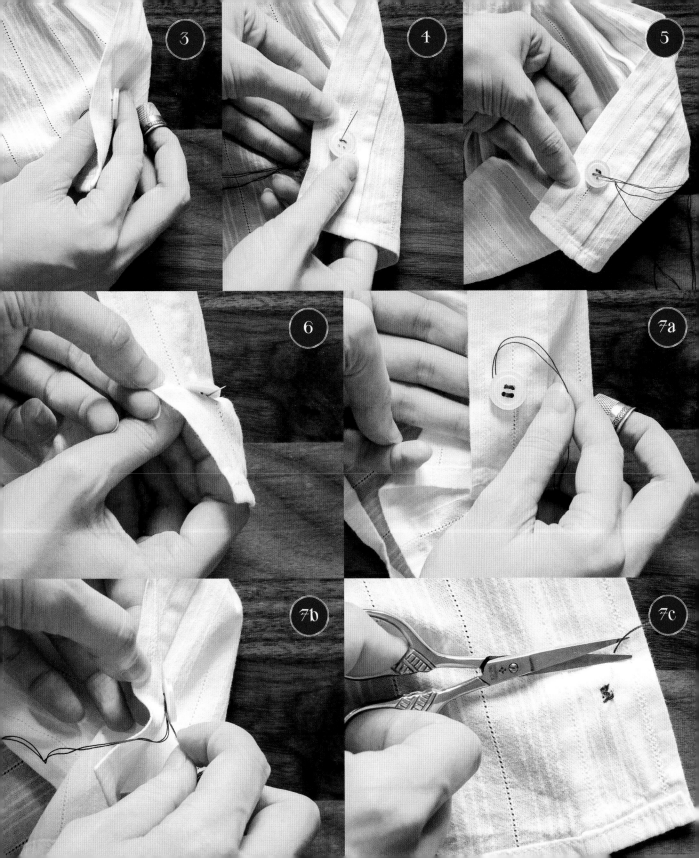

Shank Buttons

Buttons that have already been made with a shank on the back will not need the thread post added to them when sewing, so the reattaching of these is very straightforward.

Suggested Materials

Needle

Thread (strong thread such as buttonhole twist is recommended)

Wax (if desired)

Thimble

Buttons of your choosing

Scissors

1. Using a strong doubled thread, anchor your stitch (page 50) on the wrong side of the garment, burying the tail between the two layers of material if possible.

2. Positioning your button in place, bring the needle up to the right side of the garment and through the shank of the button.

3. Bring your needle back down to the wrong side of the material, securing the button to the fabric. Repeat this process several times until the button is securely fastened.

4. Finish off your thread on the wrong side of the garment with a knot or backstitch (page 59) as you prefer, and bury the tail of this between the two layers of material if possible.

Conclusion

We often ask ourselves, perhaps a bit warily: What can we *really* do to make the biggest impact on the fight against fast fashion, and to opt instead for *slow* fashion? How do we, as individuals with limited power and means, manage to have any effect on such a pervasive global industry? The first thing to remember is that fighting the entirety of fast fashion is not your responsibility to battle alone; for better or for worse, no matter how much of a model anti-fast-fashion citizen we attempt to be, none of us can single-handedly save the world. And so, while we can and should feel power in adopting whatever strategies are feasible for us in the fight against fast fashion—because they *will* collectively make a difference—we shouldn't feel burdened with the pressure of needing to adopt practices that put us beyond our realistic means. The second thing to know is that, while many anti-fast-fashion solutions will add substantial expense to one's lifestyle, the most impactful way to fight fast fashion will actually *save* you money. Although having your clothes custom-made or spending your valuable time hand-making yourself a whole wardrobe will certainly have a more positive effect than buying from high street shops, the practice of buying fewer or no new items, instead opting to repurpose and buy or trade secondhand, is what makes the biggest difference. You may be doing this already. Buying used, trading with friends, upcycling and mending what you already have all immensely reduce our consumption of new materials and signal to mass manufacturers that their overproduction efforts are not wanted.

It is worth keeping in mind the difference between being a caretaker versus being a consumer. Consumerism makes sense within the context of products that are, well, meant to be *consumed*: food, drinks, soap, and so on. Textiles—and clothing as a result—are not easy to consume, and so they must by default fall into the caretaker category: Once a garment enters our lives, we become responsible for it, including taking on the task of helping it on to the next stage of its life when we no longer have a want or purpose for it. Whether that is selling or giving it to the next caretaker, as we do with antiques and vintage items, or whether that is repurposing it into something else that can be used, assuming responsibility for items at every stage of their lives is no menial task—nor should it be. We shouldn't take on the responsibility of more items than we are capable of using, repurposing and rehoming safely.

But there is a wholly more personal benefit to the concept of paying closer attention to your wardrobe: Far from a superficial and shallow self-interest, as "fashion" is so often labeled, your clothes are the first thing that the world sees of you, and the first impression that people have of your character before you even open your mouth to introduce yourself. Your clothes can help paint a clear picture of who you are and can help you communicate to the world what you're about. You're far more likely to attract the people who understand your particular brand of weirdness—who will comfortably permit you to be your true, weirdest self without suppression—if they're able to instantly recognize a similar brand of weirdness, that they, too, have in themselves.

Go forth and make stuff.

Glossary

Armscye—The armhole of a garment, onto which a sleeve may be attached.

Backstitch—A strong constructional stitch that travels backward to meet the last stitch before traveling forward again. (See page 59 for demonstration.)

Bias—The 45-degree angle between the straight grain and the cross grain of the fabric. The bias grain generally gives a bit of stretch.

Buttonhole Stitch—A stitch usually worked along the edge of the material and that produces a series of knots; often used to strengthen the buttonhole slit. (See page 99 for demonstration.)

Cabbage—Term used historically to refer to off-cut fabric scraps, and that is most definitely superior to "scraps."

Calico—(See Muslin).

Catch Stitch—(See Cross Stitch).

Combination Stitch—Also called a running backstitch: A stitch that combines the speed of a running stitch with the strength of a backstitch. (See page 61 for demonstration.)

Cross Grain—The warp direction on the fabric, or the direction that runs parallel to the raw edge cut from the bolt.

Cross Stitch—Also known as catch stitch or herringbone stitch. This stitch is made from two parallel rows of small backstitches worked simultaneously to form a cross-pattern with the thread. (See page 66 for demonstration.)

Felling Stitch—(See Whipstitch).

Grain—Refers to direction in a fabric: straight vs cross vs bias grains.

Half Backstitch—A slightly quicker alternative to a full backstitch, in which the needle is only brought halfway back to the previous stitch for each forward stitch. (See page 60 for demonstration.)

Herringbone Stitch—(See Cross Stitch).

Muslin—Plain, unbleached cotton cloth that is usually inexpensive to obtain in bulk and that can be used for draping and mockups.

Pile—A portion of the weave of the fabric that has been cut to stand away from the fabric, creating the characteristic soft texture of velvet and velveteen.

Pin Tucks—Narrow pleats or tucks that add decoration to a garment. (See page 141 for demonstration.)

Running Stitch—A simple constructional stitch in which the needle travels in a straight, regular, forward motion. (See page 55 for demonstration.)

Selvedge—The finished edge of the material, running parallel to the warp.

Smocking—A method for gathering material in a visually pleasing pattern and that also allows for some elasticity to be worked into nonstretch materials. (See page 145 for demonstration.)

Straight Grain—The warp direction on the fabric, or the direction that runs parallel to the selvedge. This is the stronger grain and usually runs vertically along the body in finished garments.

Twill—A type of weave that produces a diagonally striped texture on a fabric.

Warp—The vertical yarns in a woven cloth, or those that run parallel to the selvedge; otherwise known as the straight grain.

Weft—The horizontal yarns in a woven cloth, those that pass over and under the warp yarns, and that run parallel to the edge cut from the bolt. Otherwise known as the cross grain.

Whipstitch—A stitch that travels in a corkscrew direction. (See page 63 for demonstration.)

Worked Bar—Thread strands reinforced usually with buttonhole stitches, and that can be used as belt loops, hook points or bars to strengthen weak junctions on a garment. (See page 120 for demonstration.)

End Notes

1   Iman Ghosh, "A Global Breakdown of Greenhouse Gas Emissions by Sector," Visual Capitalist, published November 6, 2020, https://www.visualcapitalist.com/a-global-breakdown-of-greenhouse-gas-emissions-by-sector/.

2   Laura I. Baldt, *Lippincott's Home Manuals: Clothing for Women: Selection, Design and Construction* (Philadelphia and London, J. B. Lippincott Company, 1916), 8.

3   Some beginner-friendly sources to look at for more detailed information on the weaving process include G. H. Oelsner, *Handbook of Weaves* (Garden City, NY: Dover Publications, 2011); Amanda Johnston, *Fabric for Fashion: The Complete Guide* and *Fabric for Fashion: the Swatch Book* (London: Laurence King Publishing, 2014); Irene Emery, *The Primary Structures of Fabrics: An Illustrated Classification* (New York: Thames & Hudson, 2009).

4   An example can be seen on the c. 1760–85 pair of smooth-covered court stays on pages 89–91 of *Patterns of Fashion 5*. Janet Arnold, Jenny Tiramani, Luca Costigliolo, Sébastien Passot, Armelle Lucas and Johannes Pietsch, *Patterns of Fashion 5: The Content, Cut Construction and Context of Bodies, Stays, Hoops and Rumps c. 1595–1795* (London: School of Historical Dress, 2018).

5   See, for example, extant silk yardages in the collection at the Metropolitan Museum of Art: 62.136.1 (1748, 19½ inches [49.5 cm]) and 2004.415 (1752, 19 inches [48.5 cm]). And numerous examples of short-width silks in Natalie Rothstein, *The Victoria & Albert Museum's Textile Collection: Woven Textile Design in Britain from 1750 to 1850* (London: Canopy Books, 1994). A 15½-inch (39-cm) example can be found on page 14. See Natalie Rothstein, "Dutch Silks—An Important but Forgotten Industry of the 18th Century or a Hypothesis?" *Oud Holland* 79, no. 3 (1964): 152–71, accessed July 30, 2021, http://www.jstor.org/stable/42712157 for several examples of Dutch silks ranging in width from 16¾ to 17½ inches (42.5 to 44.5 cm).

6   Baldt, 12–13, provides a suggested list of wardrobe items for the female working professional, with guidance as to how many of which items to obtain and whether these should be homemade or ready-to-wear. For example, a total of 22 tops (including waists, blouses and shirts), 3 skirts and 6 day dresses are to be accumulated over a period of three years—and this is well into the era of ready-to-wear; previous decades and centuries, especially prior to the introduction of the sewing machine in the 1850s would, theoretically, have even smaller wardrobes.

7   Much of sewing instruction today is concerned with what is "good" vs "bad" practice, the "right" vs the "wrong" way to sew, and specific measurements for thread lengths in hand sewing is a subject that many modern makers have *deep feelings* about. To this, I raise the documentation of tailors and professional makers sewing with "too-long" threads across centuries (see, for example, *Die Hausbürcher der Nürnberger Zwölfbrüderstiftungen*, Landauer I, 1511, Amb.279.2 Folio 83 recto, https://www-nuernberger--hausbuecher-de.translate.goog/75-Amb-2-279-83-r/data?_x_tr_sl=de&_x_tr_tl=en&_x_tr_hl=en-GB&_x_tr_pto=ajax,se,elem,sc), and to which I say: as long as it gets the job done, you do you.

8   Bertha Banner (1898) advises that "taking up two threads and passing over two [is] the common regulation," but this is, admittedly, a bit extreme if not impossible on some thicker fabrics. If it's any reassurance, Agnes Walker (1907) asserts that "too fine stitches . . . are to be condemned" in the interest of preserving the eyesight of her

sewing pupils. It doesn't matter so much how many threads you choose to take up or pass over—how large or fine your stitches—as long as they come out looking regular and even. Bertha Banner, *Household Sewing with Home Dressmaking* (London: Longmans, Green and Co., 1898), 5–6. Agnes Walker, *Manual of Needlework and Cutting Out: Specifically Adapted for Teachers of Sewing, Students, and Pupil-Teachers,* 5th ed. (London: Blackie & Son Limited, 1907), 35.

9   Banner, 6–7.

10   "Dressmaking Up to Date." New York: The Butterick Publishing Company, 1905. 4.

11   Banner, 64.

12   An example of this can be seen on the pair of c. 1665 stays documented in Arnold, *Patterns of Fashion 5*, 13, figures 13.6–13.8.

13   Agnes Walker, *Manual of Needlework and Cutting Out: Specifically Adapted for Teachers of Sewing, Students, and Pupil-Teachers,* 159.

14   Banner, 25.

15   A Competent Committee of Home-Makers and Physicians, *Home and Health . . . Household Manual Containing Two Thousand Recipes and Helpful Suggestions on the Building and Care of the Home in Harmony with Sanitary Laws; The Preservation of Health by Clean, Consistent Living; and the Home Treatment of the More Simple Ailments and Diseases, by the Use of Natural, Rational Remedies Instead of Drugs* (California: Pacific Press Publishing Co., 1907), 167.

16   Ruth Goodman, *How to be a Victorian* (London: Penguin, 2014). 255.

17   Walker, 38.

Bibliography

A Competent Committee of Home-Makers and Physicians. *Home and Health . . . A Household Manual Containing Two Thousand Recipes and Helpful Suggestions on the Building and Care of the Home in Harmony With Sanitary Laws; The Preservation of Health by Clean, Consistent Living; and the Home Treatment of the More Simple Ailments and Diseases, by the Use of Natural, Rational Remedies Instead of Drugs.* California: Pacific Press Publishing Co., 1907.

A Lady. *The Workwoman's Guide: Containing Instructions to the Inexperienced in Cutting Out and Completing Those Articles of Wearing Apparel, &c., which are Usually Made at Home: Also, Explanations on Upholstery, Straw-platting, Bonnet-making, Knitting, &c.* London: Simpkin, Marshall and Co., 1838.

Arnold, Janet, Jenny Tiramani, Luca Costigliolo, Sébastien Passot, Lucas Armelle and Johannes Pietsch. *Patterns of Fashion 5: The Content, Cut Construction, and Context of Bodies, Stays, Hoops and Rumps c. 1595–1795.* London: School of Historical Dress, 2018.

Baldt, Laura I. *Lippincott's Home Manuals: Clothing for Women: Selection, Design and Construction.* Philadelphia & London: J. B. Lippincott Company, 1916.

Banner, Bertha. *Household Sewing with Home Dressmaking.* London: Longmans, Green and Co., 1898.

Goodman, Ruth. *How to be a Victorian.* London: Penguin, 2014.

Newton's London Journal of Arts and Sciences. UK: W. Newton, 1824.

Rothstein, Natalie. "Dutch Silks—An Important but Forgotten Industry of the 18th Century or a Hypothesis?" *Oud Holland* 79, no. 3 (1964): 152–71. Accessed July 30, 2021. http://www.jstor.org/stable/42712157.

Rothstein, Natalie. *The Victoria & Albert Museum's Textile Collection: Woven Textile Design in Britain from 1750 to 1850.* UK: Canopy Books, 1994.

Waugh, Norah. *Corsets and Crinolines.* New York: Theatre Arts Books, 1981.

Walker, Agnes. *Manual of Needlework and Cutting Out: Specifically Adapted for Teachers of Sewing, Students, and Pupil-Teachers,* 5th ed. London: Blackie & Son Limited, 1907.

Acknowledgments

To all the wonderful humans at Page Street who quite literally made this book happen, most particularly to editor Tamara Grasty and copy editor Iris Bass who are the primary reason this book is readable and not loaded with words that were irrelevant by the 18th century. To Zoey Duncan, for expert coaching: It turns out, planning for a book is nothing like planning for a YouTube video. To Amy Betts, for swooping in with photo wizardry, and Abby Cox, for all the very-much-needed Big-Sister-Author support.

The biggest thanks must also go to the illustrious essay contributors: Dandy Wellington (IG: @dandywellington, YT: Dandy Wellington), Yang Cheon Shik (IG: @yang_cheon_shik, YT: Cheon-Shik Yang 천식 양), Claudia Vogt (IG: @retroclaude, YT: Retro Claude), Sophia Khan (IG: @Sophia_Khan, blog www.romancingthesewn.com), and Embry Whitmore (IG: @bequeermakestuff, YT: Be Queer, Make Stuff), whose styles and spirits give me (and you, too, I hope) endless inspiration. Go follow all of them on all of the platforms; you will not regret it.

Very special thanks to the Mighty Beta Reader Team for lending expert eyes to the early drafts of this book. The crew at Burnley and Trowbridge, Bettina Forsberg, Kenna Libes, Noelle Paduan, Rachel Stimson and Juul Thijssen: Your expert wisdom has lent this book infinitely more dimension than I could have given it on my own. Any inaccuracies I claim as my own.

To every single one of you wonderful viewers over on YeOldeTube—you amazing, unique, creative, glorious humans—many of whom helped to shape this book with your comments, questions, messages and Instagram poll feedback. Thanks in particular to my glorious Patreon-patrons, past and present, for allowing me the security to pursue outside-of-YouTube projects such as this. You all are WONDROUS beyond belief and I don't know what I did to deserve you.

To The Chat, where great ideas are cultivated, existential screaming vented and research tangents thoroughly explored (with sources cited); i.e., among the very best of friends. Thank you for affirming my hypothesis that there is no way to write a passage on needles without it sounding like innuendo.

Most especially to my teachers and mentors: Gregg Barnes, Erin Black, Maggie Raywood, Hilary Rosenfeld, Jenny Tiramani, Therese Bruck and the eternally beloved Kitty Leech, whose unfathomable kindness and sacrifice I will probably never in this lifetime manage to repay (though hard I'll try). And to every single one of my colleagues at the School of Historical Dress, who continue to inspire me daily. Absolute LEGENDS, one and all.

And to those who taught me posthumously: Janet Arnold, Bertha Banner and Agnes Walker. I hope in turn this book is worthy enough of survival to help some wandering stitcher 120 years from now.

About the Author

Bernadette Banner is a dress historian and filmmaker best known for her YouTube channel that documents the exploration, reconstruction and interpretation of historical dress. She works primarily by hand or using period authentic machinery in her study of dress predating the widespread use of the electric sewing machine, with particular focus on English dress between 1890 and 1914. Her work simultaneously seeks to explore how historical sewing techniques and attitudes toward dress can be relearned in an effort to fight the effects of 21st-century fast fashion and mass manufacture.

After working in costume design for Broadway, Banner graduated from New York University in 2017 and began working in historical reconstruction. She currently works as an online content creator and research consultant in London.

Index